Trail Running Oregon

Help Us Keep This Guide Up to Date

Every effort has been made by the author and editors to make this guide as accurate and useful as possible. However, many things can change after a guide is published—trails are rerouted, techniques evolve, facilities come under new management, etc.

We would love to hear from you concerning your experiences with this guide and how you feel it could be improved and kept up to date. While we may not be able to respond to all comments and suggestions, we'll take them to heart and we'll also make certain to share them with the author. Please send your comments and suggestions to the following address:

The Globe Pequot Press
Reader Response/Editorial Department
P.O. Box 480
Guilford, CT 06437
editorial@globe-pequot.com
www.falcon.com

We'd love to hear from you so we can make future editions and future guides even better.

Thanks for your input, and happy travels!

A **FALCON** GUIDE®

Trail Running Series

Trail Running
Oregon

Northwest and Central Oregon's Classic Trail Runs

LIZANN DUNEGAN

FALCON®

GUILFORD, CONNECTICUT
HELENA, MONTANA

AN IMPRINT OF THE GLOBE PEQUOT PRESS

_A_**FALCON**GUIDE ®

Photos courtesy Lizann Dunegan
Text design by Casey Shain
Maps by XNR Productions Inc. © The Globe Pequot Press

Library of Congress Cataloging-in-Publication Data is available.
ISBN 0-7627-2587-7

Manufactured in the United States of America
First Edition/First Printing

Acknowledgments

Thanks to my trail partners, who ran trails with me, took photos, helped edit the manuscript, and made this book the best it could be. I can't forget to mention my two dogs, Levi and Sage, who always accompany me when I run alone and add fun and spice to my trail-running adventures. I also appreciate the patience and support my family and friends have given me while writing this book. Thanks to Scott Adams and the folks at Falcon for allowing me to write a book about what I love doing most.

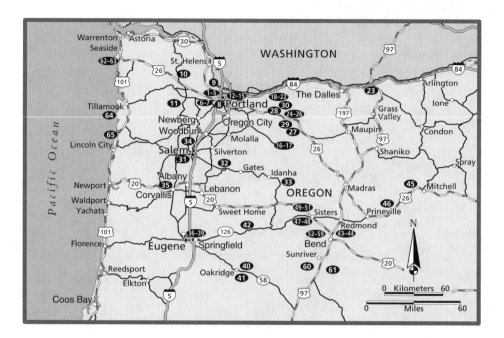

Contents

Introduction

The allure of trail running is a combination of many things: adventure, physical challenge, exploration, and an escape to the beauty of the outdoors. Trail running can be as serene or insane as you want it to be. One day you can be running on a smooth trail through old-growth trees next to a bubbling creek and the next day you can be wading through a river, trudging through knee-deep mud, hopping boulders, and jumping logs! Trail running is a great adventure that allows you to escape from the stresses in life and gives you the opportunity to refresh your mind, body, and spirit.

This book is designed for seasoned trail runners as well as newcomers who want to join in the experience. The trails in this book are varied and the scenery diverse—you'll find trails ranging from urban areas winding through cool, lush forests to those leading up high peaks with endless views. The vast majority of the trails in this book are pure dirt. Some of the urban trails, however, include sections of pavement. Many of the routes are easily within an hour's drive of some of Northwest Oregon's major cities, including Portland, Salem, Corvallis, Eugene, Hood River, Redmond, Bend, and Tillamook, and they're open year-round. Most of the routes average from 3 to 8 miles and vary widely in their level of difficulty, but all are guaranteed to be fun. If long distances are your passion, there are also routes included that are marathon length.

Trail Running Oregon is the first book written about Oregon that is specifically geared for trail runners. The trails were selected based on their fun factor, adventure potential, technical challenges, wildlife viewing, and spectacular scenery. This book includes information with each route that is runner specific, including percentage of sun exposure; trail surface (smooth or rocky); water and nature-break sources; specific trail hazards, such as bridgeless creek crossings; where the best views are; where the most running thrills can be found; and where to get the best food and drink after your run.

Northwest and Central Oregon is a trail runner's nirvana. In the heart of this nirvana is Portland, home to 5,000-acre Forest Park (one of North America's largest urban parks). Forest Park has more than 60 miles of trails and dirt roads, including the famous Wildwood Trail, which stretches through the park for more than 26 miles. In addition to Forest Park, Portland has more than fifty additional urban parks that offer a myriad of opportunities for trail runners.

Heading east of Portland, the Columbia River Gorge is filled with miles of trails that pass by billowing waterfalls, forested ridges, wildflower meadows, and beautiful creek canyons.

Hood River is the gateway to the Mount Hood National Forest, which has hundreds of miles of trails available to explore. Trail junkies can enjoy spectacular

Central Oregon is a trail runner's paradise.

views of towering 11,239-foot Mount Hood, run around high alpine lakes, and follow wild and scenic rivers.

The Willamette Valley is filled with county and state parks that offer spectacular running trails that wind through rolling farmland, along picturesque creeks with
magnificent waterfalls, and through mossy, old-growth forest.

Central Oregon is a trail runner's dream come true. This land of volcanoes is
filled with opportunities for adventure: the sagebrush and juniper lands of Smith
Rock State Park, the ponderosa pine forests and peaks surrounding the western
town of Sisters, the Painted Hills outside of Prineville, and the spectacular alpine
forests and lakes that surround the magnificent Central Oregon Cascade volcanoes
outside of Bend.

The Oregon Coast also presents trail runners with plenty of terrain to explore.
You can run through a mystical coastal forest, head out to the tip of Cape Lookout,
or run on a long sandy beach next to crashing waves and fresh Pacific wind.

The great thing about trail running is its utter simplicity. All you need is a good
pair of trail-running shoes and that's about it. You pick the route and you go. It's as
easy as that. So lace up your shoes and use this book to find your own trail-running
adventure in Northwest and Central Oregon!

The Art of Trail Running

Getting Started

If you are new to trail running, begin by selecting a popular trail with modest elevation gain and a high percentage of smooth trail surface. Trail running requires more
concentration than running on pavement. Focus on upcoming trail obstacles and
concentrate on your foot placement. Try your first trail run on a day with good
weather. Begin with a slow, easy pace to warm up and then increase your speed
based on your fitness level. Combine running with walking breaks. Slowly over several weeks increase your distance and running time. Once you feel comfortable running thirty to forty minutes on flat terrain, pick a trail that has some technical
obstacles (roots, rocks, mud) and elevation gain. Keep your feet high as you move
through awkward terrain. Budding trail runners have a heightened risk of taking
falls. If you feel a fall coming, look for the softest place to land, keep your hands
close to your chest, and try to roll into the fall with a large part of your body to
absorb the shock. Also, before you head out on a trail run, always make sure you
have plenty of daylight and bring along a partner.

How to Handle Hills

It's pretty hard to avoid hills in Northwest and Central Oregon. For some, blasting
up and down hills is the spice of trail running. Slowly acclimate to running hills by
choosing routes with modest elevation gain. When you're ascending a hill, slow your
speed, keep an erect posture, use your arms to help "power" you up the hill, shorten
your stride, and maintain a regular breathing rhythm. If you become short of breath,
slow down—it will be easier next time. For many trail runners, speed walking up a
steep grade is faster and takes less effort than trying to run. Once you reach the top
of the hill, you're ready for one of the most exciting parts of trail running—the
downhill! When you descend moderate hills, keep your weight back with your knees
slightly bent, take small steps, and use your arms for balance. If you are on a really
steep descent, you can slalom downhill like a skier if the trail is wide enough. You
can also try descending with a skipping type motion. Apply your braking action
when your feet are together—this allows you to maintain your balance if your feet
slide and prevents you from doing the splits if you wipe out.

Shoes and Socks

There are dozens of different types of trail-running shoes currently on the market. If you already own a pair of road-running shoes or cross-training shoes, these will work fine for most smooth trails. Good trail-shoe characteristics include a tough sole, wide heel profile, toe guard, and high-profile rand. Trail shoes protect your feet from impact, have good stability, and help keep your feet dry when running through wet terrain. Purchase a shoe that is a half-size larger than your normal street footwear. When you run for long periods of time over technical terrain, your feet swell—buying shoes a half-size larger allows room for this swelling and will cut down on your chances of getting blisters. The socks you choose to wear are also another important consideration. Steer clear of cotton socks and instead use socks made of wool or a synthetic blend. These socks provide better cushioning, wick moisture away from your feet, and help prevent blisters.

Clothing

The weather in Northwest and Central Oregon is typically wet and cold during the winter and spring months and drier in the summer and fall. The best way to combat the outdoor elements is to dress in layers. Wear a wicking layer next to your skin, and then, depending on how cold it is, the next layer can be a fleece jacket or vest. If it's wet out, your outer layer should be waterproof and breathable. A hat and gloves may also be advisable depending on how cold it is. Avoid cotton at all costs. It doesn't keep moisture from your skin, or dry very fast, and it can quickly make you cold. During the summer and fall when the weather is drier, synthetic shorts and tops work well. Shorts made specifically for trail running often feature different types of pockets that come in handy for stashing trail food and keys. If you are running in the mountains, bring a fleece or wool layer, and a waterproof jacket if the weather looks questionable. Ankle gaiters also help keep snow, pebbles, scree, and dirt out of your shoes.

Eating and Drinking

Eating enough calories and staying hydrated is key to a trail runner's happiness. Bring water during the summer season and on routes longer than an hour. Bicycle water bottles or hydration packs are the easiest to carry. For routes longer than an hour, you may want to substitute a sports drink for water. These drinks give you an energy boost and help replace lost electrolytes. Don't be tempted to drink directly out of a stream no matter how clean it looks. Carry a lightweight water filter or iodine tablets to purify stream water from contaminants such as Giardia and bacteria.

The unfortunate trail runner who contracts Giardia can experience severe cramping, diarrhea, vomiting, and fatigue about two weeks after exposure. If you experience these symptoms, be sure to visit a doctor as soon as possible to receive treatment. There are a variety of sports bars and gels on the market that can easily be stashed in your pocket or pack that provide the calories you need to have a fun run. Other trail food that you may want to bring includes gorp, raisins, dried fruit, bagels, chocolate bars, and peanut butter and jelly sandwiches. A good natural food is a banana. Although it won't hold up well on the trail, it makes a great snack before or after a trail run.

Weather

The weather in Northwest and Central Oregon varies depending on what area you're visiting. In the Willamette Valley, the western edge of the Columbia River Gorge, and the coast, you can expect rain, rain, and more rain beginning in November and lasting often through June. All this rain means that many trails in the winter can be muddy and wet. If you are prepared for these conditions, you'll find that running during the winter months means fewer people and more solitude. July through October promises the best dry running days.

Expect snow above 4,000 feet on Cascade Mountain routes beginning in late October and sometimes lasting through the end of June. Snowfall is possible at any time of year above this elevation. Many of the high mountain and lake trails do not open until July depending on the depth of the snowpack.

Hood River and Central Oregon are much drier and sunnier than the Willamette Valley and the coast. If you want to escape the rain and clouds in the Willamette Valley and the coast, head to Central Oregon and check out some of the trails around Bend, Redmond, Prineville, and Sisters.

Hypothermia

Hypothermia occurs when the body cannot generate enough heat to maintain normal body temperature. This condition usually strikes when the body's energy reserves are depleted, the weather turns nasty, and the runner does not have adequate layers to stay warm. Symptoms can appear slowly and may include cold, pale skin, shivering, decreased coordination, and slurred speech and vision. To treat hypothermia get the runner into a warm, dry place indoors. Remove wet clothing and dress the runner in dry clothes, including a hat and mittens. Also make sure the runner receives large quantities of warm liquids. To avoid hypothermia, carry extra clothing and plenty of food and water, and check the weather forecast before heading out.

View of the Clackamas River

Dehydration and Heat Exhaustion

If you are heading out for a run on a hot day, make sure you are well hydrated before you start. Bring your water bottle filled with electrolyte solution, and wear light-colored breathable clothing, a hat, sunglasses, and sunscreen. If you experience a headache, sudden fatigue, or decreased coordination and judgment during your run, you are most likely dehydrated. A more serious condition is heat exhaustion. Symptoms of heat exhaustion include cramps, nausea, profuse sweating, weakened pulse, and light-headedness. If you or your trail partner experience dehydration or heat exhaustion, lay down in a shady area, loosen your clothing, and drink large quantities of an electrolyte solution (if available) or water. Rest until the symptoms begin to subside.

Getting Lost

Before heading out prep yourself with the trail directions and carry a map. If you are running in a more remote area, always inform someone of your destination and expected return time. When you are running the route, make mental notes of landmarks and major trail junctions. If you become disoriented, it's best to head back the way you came instead of forging on. You can carry a cell phone but it may not work in remote areas.

Bears

Bears generally avoid people. They do not like to be surprised and they are very protective of their young. If you suspect a bear is in the area (you see scat droppings on the trail, you are in a thick berry patch, or you have heard reports of bears in the area), make noise prior to sweeping around bends. You'll most likely never see a bear but if you have an encounter slowly retreat and do not turn your back. Clap your hands loudly and yell to deter the bear. If a bear does attack, curl up in a fetal position and play dead, or climb a tree (if it is easy to get to).

Cougars

Although cougars (also known as mountain lions or pumas) are rarely seen in Northwest and Central Oregon, it's important to know how to deal with a cougar encounter. If you see a cougar, stop and make eye contact with the animal and stand your ground. Don't turn your back and run—this will only trigger the cougar's instinct to chase you and hunt you down. Make yourself appear larger by spreading your arms, waving your coat, or throwing rocks or branches. Speak loudly or yell to discourage the animal from treating you as weak prey.

Trail Ethics

As a runner you should yield to hikers, backpackers, and horses. When you are coming up behind a hiker, let the person know you are coming by saying "on your left." Be sure to thank folks for stepping aside. If you encounter horses, stop, quietly step off the trail, and wait for the horse and rider to pass. If you are running uphill, you should yield to runners coming downhill. If you are running on a trail you are sharing with a mountain biker, theoretically the mountain biker should yield to you. Frequently, though, it's easier for the trail runner to step off the trail, especially for a large group of mountain bikers.

Wilderness Restrictions/Regulations

The Bureau of Land Management and the U.S. Forest Service manage most of the public lands in Northwest and Central Oregon. Trailhead fees are $5.00 per day, or you can buy an annual Northwest Forest Pass for $30.00, which is good at all participating national forests and scenic areas in Oregon and Washington. You can find participating national forests and locations for purchasing a Northwest Forest Pass by calling (800) 270–7504 or going online to www.naturenw.org.

A majority of Oregon's state parks require a $3.00 day-use pass, or you can purchase a $30.00 State Park annual pass. If you are running trails on the Oregon Coast, you can also purchase an Oregon Pacific Coast Passport. This passport is valid for entrance, day use, and vehicle parking fees at all state and federal fee sites along the entire Oregon portion of the Pacific Coast Scenic Byway (U.S. Highway 101) from Astoria to

Negotiating a boulder problem

Brookings. An annual passport, valid for the calendar year, is available for $35. A five-consecutive-day passport is available for $10. Call (800) 551–6949 to purchase an Oregon State Park pass or Oregon Pacific Coast Passport.

Before you head out to explore Northwest and Central Oregon's trails, find out what type of permits and restrictions are in place for the area you are going to visit.

How to Use This Book

Run Descriptions

Each route includes a topographical map, elevation profile, photo, and at-a-glance information that will help you pick out the trail that best fits your mood and ability. Below is a quick explanation of the different information components you'll find in each route.

Route number, name, and region/area: The routes have been numbered based on the region of Northwest and Central Oregon where they are found. The name of the route is often the actual name of a specific trail or the area where the trail is found. The regions/areas have been organized as follows: Portland; Columbia River Gorge; Hood River/Mount Hood; the Willamette Valley towns of Salem, Corvallis, Eugene, and Oakridge; the Central Oregon towns of Redmond, Prineville, Sisters, and Bend; and the Oregon Coast.

Pain: This measure tells you the route's difficulty based on a scale of 1 to 5, with 1 being the easiest and 5 being the most difficult. This measure was determined by a combination of the route's steepness, technical obstacles (roots, rocks, logs, stream crossings), and distance.

Gain: This rather subjective measure tells you how awesome a trail is based on a scale of 1 to 5, with 1 being the lowest and 5 the highest. This measure was determined based on the opportunity for challenge and adventure, viewing potential for spectacular scenery and wildlife, and most important—how fun the trail is!

Distance: The distances were calculated using a mountain bike cyclometer on some trails and a pedometer on others. Distances on maps and posted signs don't always agree, so use the mileages as a general guide to expected landmarks and trail junctions.

Elevation gain: The total amount of feet from the route's low point to its high point.

Time: The estimated time range it will take for you to complete the route. This estimate can vary depending on the length, steepness, and technical difficulty (roots, rocks, logs, stream crossings) of the route.

The route: At-a-glance information about the trail's terrain (mountains, forest, desert, beach, etc.) and information about its obstacles (bridges, steps, wood ramps, etc.) as well as the types of views present. It also lists if the route is singletrack or doubletrack. (**Note:** Singletrack refers to a trail that is wide enough for one person. Doubletrack refers to routes that are usually old roadbeds originally built for vehicles.)

Trail surface: Whether you'll be running on a smooth, flat surface or a rocky, root-strewn one is important to know before you pick a route. This statistic gives you an estimated percent of smooth dirt, rockiness, and pavement that is present on a route. The rockiness percentage refers to loose or embedded rocks that are large enough to require careful foot placements.

Sun exposure: Estimate of what percentage of the trail is sunny. Knowing how much sun exposure you'll get on a trail and being prepared, such as by bringing water and wearing sunscreen, can greatly increase the fun factor of your run.

Runability: Estimated percentage of the trail that the average trail runner should be able to run and not walk. Steep routes, creek crossings, and very rocky terrain are examples of terrain where a runner would prefer to walk.

Season: Lists the time of the year the route is open. Most of the trails are open year-round. Trails in the mountains are usually snowed in during the winter season.

Other users: Describes other types of users you may find on the trail—mountain bikers, hikers, or equestrians.

Canine compatibility: Lists if dogs are permitted on the trail.

Permits/fees: Lists any permits or fees that are required by governing agencies to use the trail or park at the trailhead. For more information on the Northwest Forest Pass visit www.naturenw.org and www.freeourforests.org. For more information on Oregon state parks visit www.oregonstateparks.org.

Trail contact: Includes the name, address, phone number, and Web site (if available) of the organization responsible for trail maintenance and information.

Maps: Contains a list of maps pertinent to the route.

Trail scoop: Provides a brief summary of trail highlights and specific hazards you need to be aware of.

Finding the trailhead: Provides driving directions to the trailhead.

Trail dirt: Provides detailed mile by mile route directions. In addition, descriptions are given for awesome views, fun downhills, killer uphills, easy-to-miss turns, helpful landmarks, water sources, and rest rooms. Everything you need to know to have fun and finish the route is included here.

Trail food: Lists local eateries that serve good, fulfilling food and drink that will satisfy your hungry stomach after a good run.

Map Legend

═══════	Limited access highway
═(14)═	Provincial highway
──────	Other road
══════	Light duty road
= = = = =	Unimproved road
▬▬▬▬▬	Featured trail
- - - - -	Other trail
··············	Low tide route
+++++++	Railroad
•——•——•	Powerline
⌐ _ _ ¬	Parks
ⅢⅢ	Steps
▲	Campground or site
∬	Falls
•—•	Gate
≍	Bridge
◻	Overlook/viewpoint
℗	Parking
▲	Peak
■	Point of interest
START	Trailhead

Runs at a Glance

Runs by Pain (Difficulty)

Rating #1

    Banks–Vernonia State Trail

    Cannon Beach

    Deschutes River State Park Loop

    Eagle Rock Loop

    Fall River

    First Street Rapids

    Lost Lake Loop

    Glendoveer Fitness Trail Loop

    McKenzie River

    Minto–Brown Island Park Loop

    Oaks Bottom Wildlife Refuge

    Suttle Lake Loop

    Warrior Rock Lighthouse

    Willamette Mission State Park Loop

Rating #2

    Canyon Creek Meadows Loop

    Cape Kiwanda

    Deschutes River Trail

    Ecola State Park to Indian Beach

    Leif Erikson Drive

    Mirror Lake Loop

    Mount Tabor Loop

    Pamelia Lake

    Powell Butte Nature Park Loop

    Riverside Trail

    Salmon Creek

    Shevlin Park Loop

    Steins Pillar

    Tamanawas Falls

    Timothy Lake Loop

    Tryon Creek State Park Loop

    Tumalo Falls

    West Metolius River

Rating #3

Cape Lookout
Carroll Rim–Painted Hills Overlook
Clackamas River
Dan's Trail
Eagle Creek
East Fork of Hood River
Leif Erikson Drive–Wildwood Loop
Lower Macleay Park to Pittock Mansion
Marquam Nature Park Loop
Marquam Shelter to Council Crest
Mount Pisgah Arboretum Loop
Park Meadow
Paulina Lake Loop
Ridgeline Trail: Spencer Butte to Blanton Road
Ridgeline Trail Loop: Spencer Butte to Fox Hollow Road
Salmon River
Silver Falls State Park Loop
Wildwood–Wild Cherry Loop
Wildwood Trail to Pittock Mansion

Rating #4

Angels Rest
Black Butte
Hagg Lake Loop
Horsetail–Ponytail–Oneonta–Triple Falls
Larison Creek
Mount Pisgah Summit
Pilot Butte State Park
Smith Rock State Park Loop
Tam McArthur Rim
Vista Ridge–Cairn Basin–Eden Park Loop
Wahkeenah Falls Loop

Rating #5

Gray Butte to Smith Rock State Park
Green Lakes Loop
Larch Mountain

Runs by Gain (Fun Factor and Aesthetic Appeal)

Rating #1
Banks–Vernonia State Trail
Willamette Mission State Park Loop

Rating #2
Dan's Trail
First Street Rapids
Glendoveer Fitness Trail Loop
Leif Erikson Drive
Marquam Nature Park Loop
Minto–Brown Island Park Loop
Mount Pisgah Summit
Oaks Bottom Wildlife Refuge
Powell Butte Nature Park Loop
Steins Pillar

Rating #3
Cannon Beach
Cape Lookout
Carroll Rim–Painted Hills Overlook
Deschutes River State Park Loop
East Fork of Hood River
Ecola State Park to Indian Beach
Fall River
Hagg Lake Loop
Leif Erikson Drive–Wildwood Loop
Marquam Shelter to Council Crest
Mount Pisgah Arboretum Loop
Mount Tabor Loop
Pilot Butte State Park
Ridgeline Trail: Spencer Butte to Blanton Road
Ridgeline Trail Loop: Spencer Butte to Fox Hollow Road
Salmon Creek
Shevlin Park Loop
Suttle Lake Loop
Tamanawas Falls
Tryon Creek State Park Loop

Vista Ridge–Cairn Basin–Eden Park Loop
Warrior Rock Lighthouse
Wildwood–Wild Cherry Loop
Wildwood Trail to Pittock Mansion

Rating #4

Angels Rest
Black Butte
Canyon Creek Meadows Loop
Cape Kiwanda
Clackamas River
Deschutes River Trail
Eagle Rock Loop
Gray Butte to Smith Rock State Park
Horsetail–Ponytail–Oneonta–Triple Falls
Larison Creek
Lost Lake Loop
Lower Macleay Park to Pittock Mansion
McKenzie River
Mirror Lake Loop
Park Meadow
Paulina Lake Loop
Riverside Trail
Salmon River
Silver Falls State Park Loop
Timothy Lake Loop
Tumalo Falls

Rating #5

Eagle Creek
Green Lakes Loop
Larch Mountain
Pamelia Lake
Smith Rock State Park Loop
Tam McArthur Rim
Wahkeenah Falls Loop
West Metolius River

Portland

As the largest city in Oregon, Portland has thousands of acres of parks and preserves that have hundreds of miles of fun singletrack trails waiting to be explored. A well-known park is 5,000-acre Forest Park—one of the world's largest city parks. This magnificent park rests right in the heart of the city limits and is filled with beautiful forest trails that wind through Portland's West Hills and along the spine of the Tualatin Mountains. The most well-known trail in the park is Wildwood Trail. This gorgeous singletrack trail sweeps through emerald forest for more than 26 miles. Two recommended routes that travel over some of the most scenic sections of this trail are Wildwood Trail to Pittock Mansion and the Wildwood–Wild Cherry Loop. Marquam Nature Park is another notable destination you should add to your trail list on the west side of town. Hill runners will enjoy the challenge of the Marquam Nature Trail, which climbs 600-plus feet through a forested canyon to Council Crest Park. This park has one of the best views of the city from its 1,043-foot summit. Tryon Creek State Park is another west-side park that features more than 14 miles of interconnecting trails. Picturesque Tryon Creek wanders through the heart of this park. Many singletrack trails follow the course of the creek and take you over rolling terrain past immense red cedar, Douglas fir, and big-leaf maple trees. The east side of the city is host to two beautiful forested parks that are located atop extinct volcanic buttes. Powell Butte Nature Park and Mount Tabor Park give trail-running enthusiasts many miles of singletrack that weave through shady forest, offering opportunities for lung-bursting hill workouts and phenomenal views of Portland and Mount Hood. Two classic river trails that should not be missed are the Clackamas River Trail and the Riverside Trail located an hour east of the city in the Mount Hood National Forest. These two gorgeous river trails take you through mossy old-growth forest, past secluded swimming holes and spectacular viewpoints of the Clackamas River.

1: Lower Macleay Park to Pittock Mansion

Region/area:	Portland
Pain:	3
Gain:	4
Distance:	3.8 miles out and back
Elevation gain:	600 feet
Time:	45 minutes to 1.25 hours
The route:	Dirt and paved trails that travel next to bubbling Balch Creek through a fantastic forest setting in Macleay Park and Forest Park. City and mountain views. Bridge crossings.
Trail surface:	70% smooth dirt, 15% rocky, 15% paved
Sun exposure:	10%
Runability:	100%
Season:	Year-round
Other users:	Hikers
Canine compatibility:	Leashed dogs permitted
Permits/fees:	None
Trail contact:	Portland Parks & Recreation, Portland, OR, (503) 823–PLAY, www.parks.ci.portland.or.us
Maps:	USGS Portland (7.5' series); *Forest Park, One City's Wilderness,* printed by the Oregon Historical Society, (503) 306–5233, www.ohs.org

Trail scoop: This forest escape begins at Lower Macleay Park, located in Northwest Portland, and winds its way up Balch Creek Canyon for almost a mile to Upper Macleay Park through a second-growth forest of Douglas fir, western red cedar, and big-leaf maple. The first half of the route you'll pass by big rock pools that are haven to wild trout and wild raspberries, maidenhair fern, and vine maple. Brightly colored wildflowers line the trail with their unique beauty. At Upper Macleay Park you'll cross Cornell Road and then continue your uphill odyssey through a fern-filled forest to the parklike grounds of the historic Pittock Mansion estate. *Oregonian* editor Henry L. Pittock built this enormous house in 1914. From this stately estate you can take a breather and gaze at Portland's downtown skyline and majestic Mount Hood before retracing your route.

Finding the trailhead: From I–405 north in downtown Portland, take the Highway 30 West–St. Helens exit (#3). At the end of the off-ramp, stay in the right lane,

Cruising on the Lower Macleay Trail

which turns into Northwest Vaughn Street. Go 0.6 mile west on Northwest Vaughn Street. Turn left onto Northwest 28th Street and travel 1 block. Turn right onto Northwest Upshur Street and proceed 0.2 mile to a parking area at the road's end at Lower Macleay Park. *DeLorme: Oregon Atlas & Gazetteer:* Page 66 D3.

TRAIL DIRT

0.0 Start running on a wide paved path that parallels bubbling Balch Creek. (The paved trail ends after 0.2 mile.)

0.6 Pass by a historic stone house and a trail intersection. Go straight and continue running next to the creek. *(Watch out for some rough rocky sections on this part of the trail that will test your ankle strength. Also keep a keen eye out for loose dogs and their owners, who often frequent this section of the trail.)*

0.7 Cross the creek over a wood bridge and power up some steep switchbacks.

0.8 Arrive at Upper Macleay Park. Continue running on the dirt trail as it parallels the parking area at Upper Macleay Park. (There are rest rooms at Upper Macleay Park if you hear nature calling.) Cross Northwest Cornell Road and pick up the trail on the other side.

0.9 Take a very sharp right turn and continue on the Upper Macleay Trail as it sweeps uphill through a shady forest canopy.

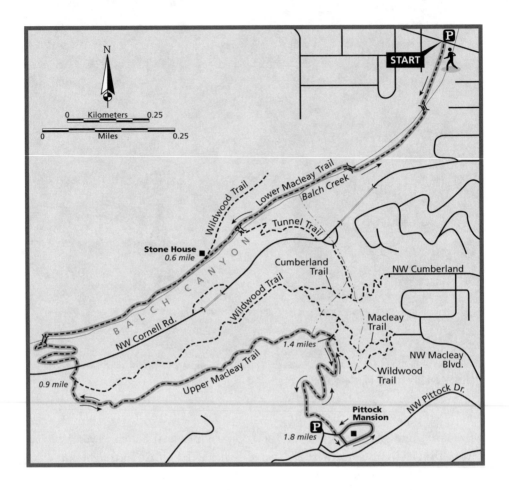

1.4 Take a sharp right turn at a four-way intersection and continue your uphill ascent on a series of steep switchbacks.

1.8 Arrive at the Pittock Mansion parking lot. Continue running on the left side of the parking lot and pick up the 0.2-mile paved path that circles the mansion. (You can quench your thirst at the drinking fountains that are located adjacent to this paved path. Public rest rooms are also available. As you continue on this short paved section, you'll arrive at a viewpoint that offers gorgeous vistas of downtown Portland and Mount Hood.)

2.0 The paved loop trail ends. Retrace the same route back to the trailhead.

3.8 Arrive back at the trailhead.

Trail running is a fast-growing sport. According to the Outdoor Recreation Coalition of America, there was a **38 percent increase** in those individuals involved in the sport of trail running between 1998 and 1999. In 1999, 6.2 million Americans identified themselves as trail runners.

TRAIL FOOD

Bridgeport Brewpub, 1313 Northwest Marshall Street, Portland, OR 97210, (503) 241–3612, bridgeportbrew.com/pubs/brewpub.html

Portland Brewing Company, 2730 Northwest 31st Avenue, Portland, OR 97210, (503) 226–7623, www.portlandbrew.com

2: Wildwood–Wild Cherry Loop

Region/area:	Portland
Pain:	3
Gain:	3
Distance:	4.8-mile loop
Elevation gain:	570 feet
Time:	45 minutes to 1 hour
The route:	This fun singletrack trail begins by paralleling Balch Creek and then travels through a shady big-leaf maple and Douglas fir canopy in Forest Park. Bridge crossings.
Trail surface:	70% smooth dirt, 10% rocky, 20% paved
Sun exposure:	20%
Runability:	100%
Season:	Year-round
Other users:	Hikers, mountain bikers (on Leif Erikson Drive only)
Canine compatibility:	Leashed dogs permitted
Permits/fees:	None
Trail contact:	Portland Parks & Recreation, Portland, OR, (503) 823–PLAY, www.parks.ci.portland.or.us
Maps:	USGS Portland (7.5' series); *Forest Park, One City's Wilderness,* printed by the Oregon Historical Society, (503) 306–5233, www.ohs.org

Wildwood Trail in Forest Park

Trail scoop: Start running upstream along the scenic Balch Creek in a dark forested canyon. Most likely you'll be sharing this attractive trail with hikers and their dogs. Hang a right at an old stone house and begin traversing the eastern Tualatin Mountain range. The crowds soon thin and the rolling elevation revs your cardio system. The trail winds along the ridges and drainages of the steep hillsides while building in altitude. Mud bogs can form in places during the wet season. After a couple miles of this enchanting trail, turn right to descend onto the popular Leif Erikson multiuse trail. This return route leads you through a historic neighborhood along paved Northwest Thurman Street for about a mile to your starting point. Rest rooms and water are available at the trailhead.

Finding the trailhead: From I–405 north in downtown Portland, take the Highway 30 West–St. Helens exit (#3). At the end of the off-ramp, stay in the right lane, which turns into Northwest Vaughn Street. Go 0.6 mile west on Northwest Vaughn Street. Turn left onto Northwest 28th Street and travel 1 block. Turn right onto Northwest Upshur Street and proceed 0.2 mile to a parking area at Lower Macleay Park. *DeLorme: Oregon Atlas & Gazetteer:* Page 66 D3.

TRAIL DIRT

0.0 From Lower Macleay Park start running on the paved path that parallels bubbling Balch Creek.

0.6 Arrive at a trail intersection just before an old stone house. Take a sharp right onto the signed Wildwood Trail.

1.2 Cross Holman Lane and continue straight on Wildwood Trail.

1.6 Cross Aspen Trail and continue straight on Wildwood Trail. (Be on the lookout for salmonberries, raspberries, and blackberries lining the trail during the summer months.)

2.8 Stay to the right and continue running on Wildwood Trail. (The signed Birch Trail goes left.)

3.2 Take a sharp right on the signed Wild Cherry Trail and start gliding downhill.

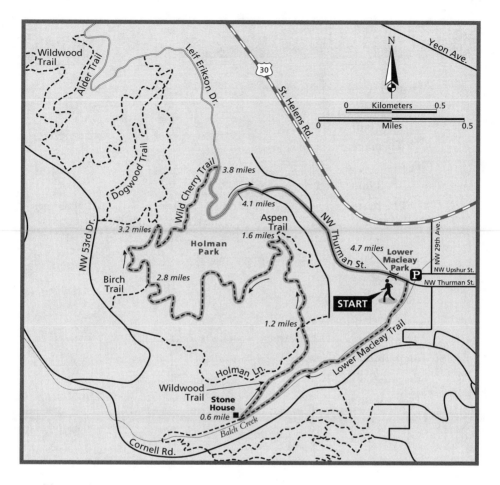

3.8 Turn right on a paved section of Leif Erikson Drive. *(Watch out for mountain bikers traveling at near warp speeds on this section of the route.)*

4.1 Leif Erikson Drive ends. (There is a water fountain here if you want a drink.) Go around a green metal gate and continue downhill on the paved Northwest Thurman Street through a historic neighborhood.

4.7 Cross the Thurman Street Bridge. (Lower Macleay Park is below the bridge.)

4.8 After you cross the bridge, look for a set of stairs on the left side of the road that will take you down to Lower Macleay Park and your starting point.

TRAIL FOOD

Acapulco's Gold, 2610 Vaughn Street, Portland, OR 97210, (503) 294–2190

Bridgeport Brewpub, 1313 Northwest Marshall Street, Portland, OR 97210, (503) 241–3612, bridgeportbrew.com/pubs/brewpub.html

Portland Brewing Company, 2730 Northwest 31st Avenue, Portland, OR 97210, (503) 226–7623, wwsw.portlandbrew.com

3: Leif Erikson Drive–Wildwood Loop

Region/area:	Portland
Pain:	3
Gain:	3
Distance:	7.9-mile loop
Elevation gain:	450 feet
Time:	1.5 to 2 hours
The route:	The route travels on singletrack trails and a doubletrack gravel road through the scenic treed setting of Forest Park. Tree roots. Bridge crossings.
Trail surface:	60% dirt, 38% gravel, 2% paved
Sun exposure:	20%
Runability:	100%
Season:	Year-round
Other users:	Hikers, mountain bikers (on Leif Erikson Drive only)
Canine compatibility:	Leashed dogs permitted
Permits/fees:	None
Trail contact:	Portland Parks & Recreation, Portland, OR, (503) 823–PLAY, www.parks.ci.portland.or.us
Maps:	USGS Linnton and Portland (7.5' series); *Forest Park, One City's Wilderness,* printed by the Oregon Historical Society, (503) 306–5233, www.ohs.org

Trail scoop: This loop route takes you on a wild and free run through the lush canopy of 5,000-acre Forest Park. A large section of this trail follows the Wildwood Trail that sweeps along the ridgeline through a predominantly big-leaf maple and Douglas fir forest, ducking in and out of side canyons and rolling up and down the fern-covered hillside. The return portion of this trail takes you along the popular Leif Erikson Drive, which is usually packed with walkers, mountain bikers, and runners. Water is available at the start of this route.

Finding the trailhead: From I–405 north in downtown Portland, take the Highway 30 West–St. Helens exit (#3). At the end of the off-ramp, stay in the right lane, which turns into Northwest Vaughn Street. At the first stoplight turn left onto Northwest 23rd Avenue. Go 1 block and turn right onto Northwest Thurman Street. Go 1.4 miles to the end of Northwest Thurman Street and park near the green metal gate. Leif Erikson Drive starts at the green metal gate. *DeLorme: Oregon Atlas & Gazetteer:* Page 66 D3.

A quiet morning run in Forest Park

TRAIL DIRT

0.0 Go around a green gate and start running on Leif Erikson Drive. (A drinking fountain is located on the right side of the trail just after you go through the green gate.)

0.3 Turn left on the signed Wild Cherry Trail and begin your uphill odyssey. *(On this path you'll have to negotiate sections of tangled tree roots that do their best to trip you up.)*

0.9 Turn right on Wildwood Trail. Begin your forest trek on this loose and lanky trail that follows the contour of the hillside through amazing forest greenery. Run about 15 feet and you'll arrive at another trail fork. Veer right and continue on Wildwood Trail.

1.5 Cross Dogwood Trail. Continue straight on Wildwood Trail. (**Bailout:** If you want to bail out now you can take a right onto Dogwood Trail, which will take you back to Leif Erikson Drive. Once you reach Leif Erikson Drive, turn right and follow it back to the trailhead.)

2.4 The trail passes Northwest 53rd Drive on your left. Continue your journey on Wildwood Trail.

2.6 Arrive at a trail intersection with Alder Trail. Continue straight on Wildwood Trail. (**Bailout:** This is your second opportunity to complete a shorter loop by turning right onto Alder Trail, which hooks up with Leif Erikson Drive. Once you reach Leif Erikson Drive, turn right and follow it back to the trailhead.)

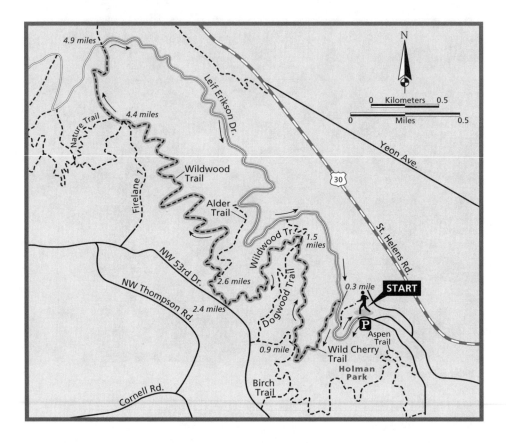

4.4 Turn right on a doubletrack road (Firelane 1) and begin a rambunctious down-hill romp.

4.9 Turn right onto Leif Erikson Drive. *(Be on the lookout for mountain bikers as they come sailing down the road.)*

7.9 Arrive at the trailhead.

TRAIL FOOD

Acapulco's Gold, 2610 Northwest Vaughn Street, Portland, OR 97210, (503) 294–2190

Bridgeport Brewpub, 1313 Northwest Marshall Street, Portland, OR 97210, (503) 241–3612, bridgeportbrew.com/pubs/brewpub.html

Portland Brewing Company, 2730 Northwest 31st Avenue, Portland, OR 97210, (503) 226–7623, www.portlandbrew.com

4: Leif Erikson Drive

Region/area:	Portland
Pain:	2
Gain:	2
Distance:	12 miles out and back (with a 22-mile option)
Elevation gain:	410 feet
Time:	2 to 4 hours depending on the length of the trail selected
The route:	Nonmotorized multiuse gravel-dirt road with distance markers that winds through 5,000-acre Forest Park in Portland. Occasional views.
Trail surface:	99% gravel, 1% pavement
Sun exposure:	40%
Runability:	100%
Season:	Year-round
Other users:	Hikers, mountain bikers
Canine compatibility:	Leashed dogs permitted
Permits/fees:	None
Trail contact:	Portland Parks & Recreation, Portland, OR, (503) 823–PLAY, www.parks.ci.portland.or.us
Maps:	USGS Linnton and Portland (7.5' series); *Forest Park, One City's Wilderness,* printed by the Oregon Historical Society, (503) 306–5233, www.ohs.org

Trail scoop: This civilized multiuse trail is an easy cruise on a multiuse gravel road that takes you through the heart of Forest Park's 5,000-acre urban sanctuary. You can keep track of your mileage by handy mileage markers that are strategically placed on the right side of the road every quarter mile. Most likely you'll encounter blazing mountain bikers doing laps on this stretch. Stay on the right side of the trail and keep an ear out for passing warnings. Water is available at the start of this route.

Finding the trailhead: From I–405 north in downtown Portland, take the Highway 30 West–St. Helens exit (#3). At the end of the off-ramp, stay in the right lane, which turns into Northwest Vaughn Street. At the first stoplight turn left onto Northwest 23rd Avenue. Proceed 1 block and turn right onto Northwest Thurman Street. Travel 1.4 miles to the end of Northwest Thurman Street and park near the green metal gate. Leif Erikson Drive starts at the green metal gate. *DeLorme: Oregon Atlas & Gazetteer:* Page 66 D3.

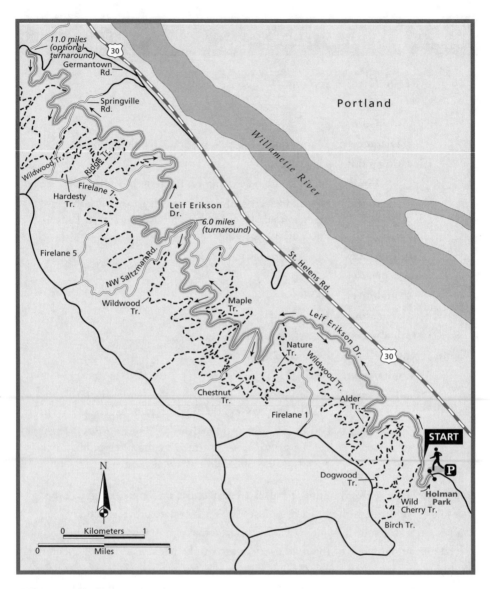

TRAIL DIRT

0.0 From the end of Northwest Thurman Street, go around a green gate and begin your fun cruise on Leif Erikson Drive. (A drinking fountain is located on the right side of the trail just after you go through the green gate.)

6.0 Arrive at a four-way intersection with Northwest Saltzman Road. This is a good turnaround point that gives you a nice 12-mile round-trip journey. (**Option:** If you are hankering for more mileage, Leif Erikson Drive continues for another 5 miles until it intersects with Northwest Germantown Road at mile 11. To continue, head straight through the four-way intersection. The road gets a bit wilder and the forest deeper on this optional section. The mileage markers soon appear only at mile intervals. A turnaround at Germantown Road would net you almost a marathon at 22 miles.)

TRAIL FOOD

Acapulco's Gold, 2610 Northwest Vaughn Street, Portland, OR 97210, (503) 294–2190

McMenamins, 1716 Northwest 23rd Avenue, Portland, OR 97210, (503) 227–0929, www.mcmenamins.com/Pubs/Tavern/index.html

5: Wildwood Trail to Pittock Mansion

Region/area:	Portland
Pain:	3
Gain:	3
Distance:	7.2 miles out and back
Elevation Gain:	200 feet
Time:	1.25 to 1.75 hours
The route:	The route starts next to the Vietnam Memorial in Washington Park, winds through Hoyt Arboretum, and then heads into Forest Park and to Pittock Mansion. City and mountain views. Bridge crossings.
Trail surface:	100% smooth dirt
Sun exposure:	5%
Runability:	100%
Season:	Year-round (the trail can be muddy during the winter months)
Other users:	Hikers
Canine compatibility:	Leashed dogs permitted
Permits/fees:	None
Trail contact:	Portland Parks & Recreation, Portland, OR, (503) 823–PLAY, www.parks.ci.portland.or.us
Maps:	USGS Portland (7.5' series); *Forest Park, One City's Wilderness,* printed by the Oregon Historical Society, (503) 306–5233, www.ohs.org

Trail scoop: This hilly route takes you along one of the most scenic sections of the

Running at Pittock Mansion

Wildwood Trail. Amazing trees surround you as you sail on the smooth route through Hoyt Arboretum. Where else can you see a grove of ancient dawn red-woods? Eventually the trail heads downhill to busy Burnside Street. After crossing Burnside you'll blast uphill through a shady canopy to your turnaround point at historic Pittock Mansion. Be sure to check out the amazing view of Portland and Mount Hood from the mansion's rear lawn. You'll follow Wildwood Trail the entire length of this route. Water and rest rooms are available at Pittock Mansion.

Finding the trailhead: From downtown Portland, head 1.8 miles west on U.S. 26 toward Beaverton. Take the exit for the Oregon Zoo and the World Forestry Center. At the end of the off-ramp, turn right onto Southwest Knights Boulevard and proceed through the Oregon Zoo parking area, following signs to the World Forestry Center. After 0.4 mile, you'll pass the World Forestry Center on your left. At 0.6 mile, turn right into a parking area directly across from the Vietnam Memorial at the intersection of Southwest Knights Boulevard and Southwest Kingston Boulevard. *DeLorme: Oregon Atlas & Gazetteer:* Page 66 D3.

TRAIL DIRT

0.0 Start running on the signed Wildwood Trail, which starts right across Knights Boulevard across from the parking area. (Don't get dazed and confused by all the trail junctions on this route—just keep your eyes peeled for the Wildwood Trail signs.)

2.8 Cross busy Burnside Street. *(Be wary of high-speed motorists rounding the bend.)*

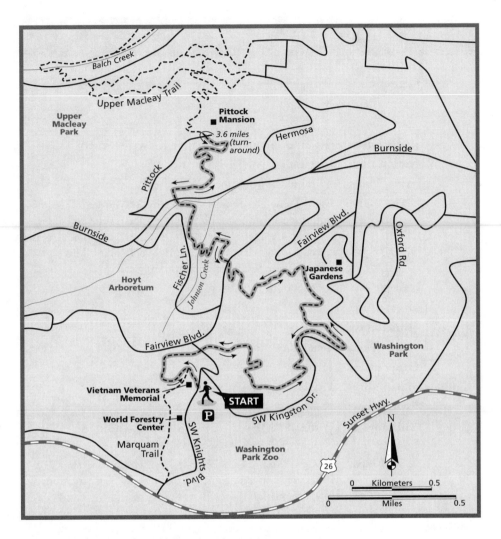

3.0 Turn left at an unsigned trail junction. Go 10 feet and stay to the left again. Get ready for a good cardio rush.

3.6 Arrive at the Pittock Mansion parking lot (your turnaround point). Retrace the same route back to the trailhead. (Water and rest rooms are adjacent to Pittock Mansion.)

7.2 Arrive back at the trailhead.

TRAIL FOOD

The Hillsdale Brew Pub, 1505 Southwest Sunset Boulevard, Portland, OR 97201, (503) 246–3938, www.mcmenamins.com/Brewing/hillsdale.html

Region/area:	Portland
Pain:	3
Gain:	3
Distance:	3.2 miles out and back
Elevation gain:	600 feet
Time:	45 minutes to 1 hour
The route:	Signed singletrack trail that begins at Marquam Shelter and travels through a picturesque Douglas fir, red alder, and big-leaf maple forest to the summit of Council Crest. Steep forest ascent and descent. Wood stairs. Three paved road crossings. City and mountain views.
Trail surface:	95% smooth dirt, 5% rocky
Sun exposure:	2%
Runability:	100%
Season:	Year-round
Other users:	Hikers
Canine compatibility:	Leashed dogs permitted
Permits/fees:	None
Trail contact:	Portland Parks & Recreation, Portland, OR, (503) 823–PLAY, www.parks.ci.portland.or.us
Maps:	USGS Portland (7.5' series); *Marquam Nature Park Trail* brochure, available from Portland Parks & Recreation, (503) 823–PLAY

Trail scoop: This trail takes you on a city escape through the fern-filled forest of Marquam Nature Park. You'll power uphill on quality dirt that twists and turns up a forested canyon to the spectacular 1,043-foot summit of Council Crest. Wild raspberries, delicate maidenhair fern, Oregon grape, elderberry, and wildflowers line the trail. Big-leaf maple and Douglas fir trees provide welcoming shade as you tackle the steep ascent. While you may think you are all alone, you'll pass by a few large West Hills homes that are tucked away in this quiet green space. After a steep romp, you'll exit the forest canopy and arrive at the summit of Council Crest. Drinking fountains at the summit provide a welcome watering hole and the inviting grassy expanse provides a great place to catch your breath. Before heading back, you might want to orient yourself to the region's geography by using the monument's landmark dial.

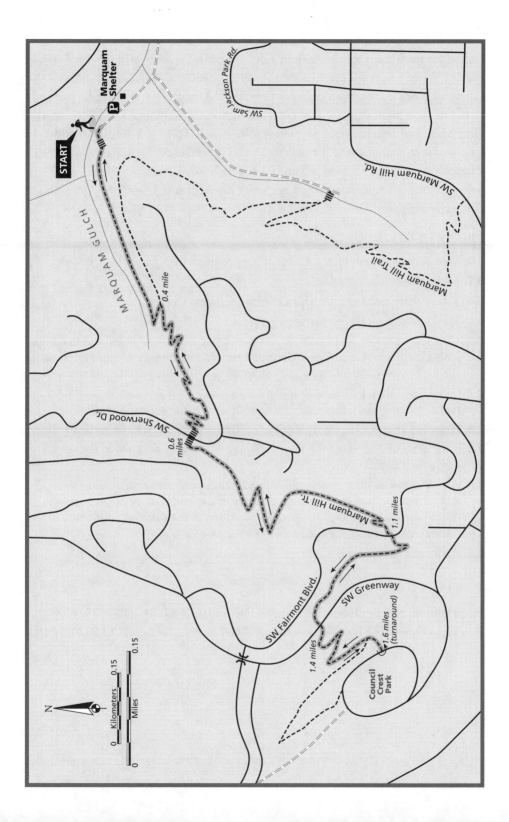

Finding the trailhead: From I–405 north in downtown Portland, take the 4th Avenue exit (#1B) and proceed 0.2 mile north. Turn left onto Southwest College Street. Proceed 1 block and turn left onto Southwest 5th Avenue. Get in the right lane and go 0.3 mile on Southwest 5th Avenue. Turn right onto Southwest Caruthers Street. Go 1 block and turn left onto Southwest 6th Avenue. Travel 0.3 mile on Southwest 6th Avenue to a stoplight at the intersection with Southwest Terwilliger Avenue. Continue straight on Southwest Sam Jackson Park Road (Southwest 6th Avenue ends here) for 0.2 mile. Just past a large water tower, turn right into the Marquam Shelter parking area. *DeLorme: Oregon Atlas & Gazetteer:* Page 60 A3.

TRAIL DIRT

0.0 Start running uphill on the trail that goes right and is signed Council Crest.

0.1 Jog up a short set of stairs.

0.4 Take a sharp right at a switchback signed Council Crest.

0.5 Turn left at a signed intersection.

0.6 Charge up a set of wood stairs. Cross Southwest Sherwood Drive and hook up with a dirt path that is signed Council Crest. Continue your summit quest as the trail crosses a small creek and continues to switchback up the canyon.

1.1 Cross Southwest Fairmont Boulevard. *(Keep an eye out for road runners and cyclists buzzing this twisty road.)* Pick up the dirt path on the other side.

1.4 Cross Southwest Greenway Avenue and charge up a dirt trail on the other side.

1.5 Turn left and exit out of the forest, running across a grassy lawn to the summit of Council Crest.

1.6 Arrive at the inviting grassy summit and a stone wall monument (your turn-around point). Soak in the gorgeous views of the Portland metro area and the distant mountain peaks, and quench your thirst at the drinking fountains. To return to the trailhead, glide back down the same route.

3.2 Arrive at the trailhead.

TRAIL FOOD

Pasta Veloce, 933 Southwest 3rd Avenue, Portland, OR 97204, (503) 223–8200

Pizzacato Gourmet Pizza, 705 Southwest Alder Street, Portland, OR 97201, (503) 226–1007

7: Marquam Nature Park Loop

Region/area:	Portland
Pain:	3
Gain:	2
Distance:	4.2-mile loop
Elevation gain:	420 feet
Time:	45 minutes to 1 hour
The route:	Signed forest path that winds through a Douglas fir and big-leaf maple forest in Marquam Nature Park. The route then hooks up with a paved pedestrian path that parallels Terwilliger Boulevard. From this path you have views of downtown Portland, the Willamette River, and Mount Hood. Bridge crossings. Wood stairs.
Trail surface:	60% smooth dirt, 40% paved
Sun exposure:	5%
Runability:	100%
Season:	Year-round
Other users:	Hikers
Canine compatibility:	Leashed dogs permitted
Permits/fees:	None
Trail contact:	Portland Parks & Recreation, Portland, OR, (503) 823–PLAY, www.parks.ci.portland.or.us
Maps:	USGS Portland (7.5' series); *Marquam Nature Park Trail* brochure, available from Portland Parks & Recreation, (503) 823–PLAY

Trail scoop: Marquam Nature Park is a hidden oasis in Portland's southwest hills. This loop trail takes you on a trek through the arboreal haven of big-leaf maple and Douglas fir trees and past a lush forest mix of ferns, vine maple, Oregon grape, and elderberry. You'll charge through this urban greenery, bounding up and down hills and over bubbling creeks, until you exit from the forest wilds to the more civilized running world, where you'll head downhill on the paved Terwilliger jogging path that will take you back to your starting point. Water is available at the trailhead.

Finding the trailhead: From I–405 north in downtown Portland, take the 4th Avenue exit (#1B) and proceed 0.2 mile north. Turn left onto Southwest College Street. Proceed 1 block and turn left onto Southwest 5th Avenue. Get in the right lane and go 0.3 mile on Southwest 5th Avenue. Turn right onto Southwest Caruthers Street.

A fun singletrack in Marquam Nature Park

Go 1 block and turn left onto Southwest 6th Avenue. Travel 0.3 mile to a stoplight at the intersection with Southwest Terwilliger Avenue. Continue straight on Southwest Sam Jackson Park Road (Southwest 6th Avenue ends here) for 0.2 mile. Just past a large water tower, turn right into the Marquam Shelter parking area. *DeLorme: Oregon Atlas & Gazetteer:* Page 60 A3.

TRAIL DIRT

0.0 Start running uphill on the trail that goes right and is signed Council Crest.

0.1 Jog up a short set of stairs.

0.4 Turn left where a sign indicates that it is 2 miles to the Terwilliger Trail. *(You'll cruise as the trail takes you over fun roller-coaster hills, but it is uneven and rocky in some sections.)*

0.7 Cross a small wooden bridge over a bubbling creek.

0.9 Continue straight (left) on the Terwilliger Trail. Go down a set of stairs to a T intersection. Turn right onto the signed Terwilliger Trail. (After this intersection the trail climbs steeply up a series of winding switchbacks.)

1.3 Arrive at a metal guardrail that parallels paved Southwest Marquam Hill Road. Turn right at the metal guardrail and run on the dirt path that parallels the guardrail. You'll arrive at a sign that reads MARQUAM TRAIL 100 YARDS. Continue running parallel to paved Southwest Marquam Hill Road. You'll pass a large water tank on your right. Right after passing the water tank, cross Southwest Marquam Hill Road and pick up the dirt trail on the other side. (From this point the trail heads downhill on a series of steep switchbacks.)

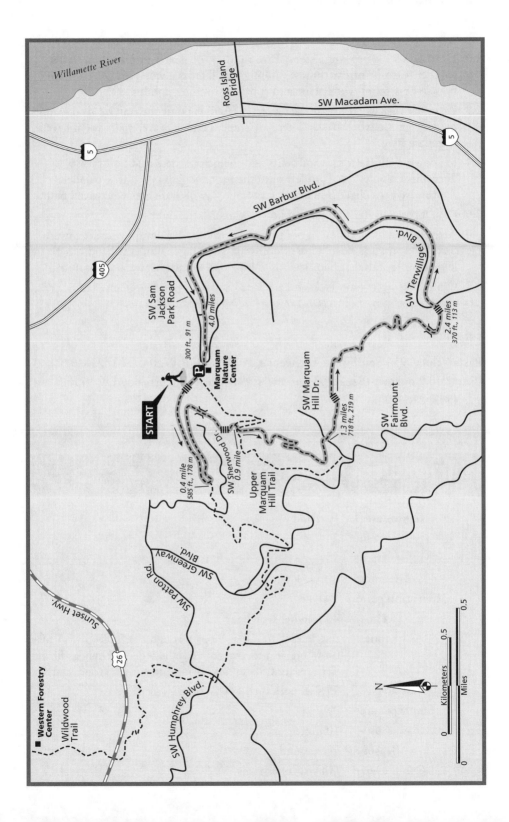

Willamette River

Ross Island Bridge

SW Macadam Ave.

SW Barbur Blvd.

SW Terwilliger Blvd.

SW Sam Jackson Park Road

4.0 miles

300 ft, 91 m

Marquam Nature Center

START

P

2.4 miles
370 ft, 113 m

SW Marquam Hill Dr.

SW Fairmount Blvd.

1.3 miles
718 ft, 219 m

0.4 mile
585 ft, 178 m

SW Sherwood Dr.
0.9 mile

Upper Marquam Hill Trail

SW Greenway Blvd.

SW Patton Rd.

Sunset Hwy.

Wildwood Trail

■ Western Forestry Center

SW Humphrey Blvd.

N

Kilometers   0.5

Miles   0.5

1.6 Head down a set of wood steps. Turn right at the next T intersection. (After another 0.1 mile of swift forest running, you'll cross a wood bridge and then muscle up a set of wood stairs and continue running uphill.)

2.3 Cross another wood bridge over a creek. (At this point the trail heads downhill on wide gentle switchbacks. There are some sections of tree roots you'll have to negotiate here.)

2.4 Jog down a short set of wood stairs and then cross the paved Southwest Terwilliger Boulevard. Turn left onto the paved jogging path that parallels Southwest Terwilliger Boulevard. Continue downhill on the wide paved path.

2.6 (You'll pass a water fountain and rest room on your right.)

4.0 Arrive at the intersection of Southwest Terwilliger Boulevard and Southwest Sam Jackson Park Road. Cross Southwest Terwilliger Boulevard and run on the left side of Southwest Sam Jackson Park Road toward Marquam Nature Park.

4.2 Cross Southwest Sam Jackson Park Road and arrive at Marquam Nature Park and your starting point. *(Use extreme caution at this road crossing!)*

TRAIL FOOD

Pasta Veloce, 933 Southwest 3rd Avenue, Portland, OR 97204, (503) 223–8200

Pizzacato Gourmet Pizza, 705 Southwest Alder Street, Portland, OR 97201, (503) 226–1007

8: Tryon Creek State Park Loop

Region/area:	Portland
Pain:	2
Gain:	3
Distance:	4-mile loop
Elevation gain:	100 feet
Time:	40 minutes to 1 hour
The route:	Singletrack trail that loops through a second-growth forest of big-leaf maple, red cedar, alder, and Douglas fir in Tryon Creek State Park. Bridge crossings. Wood stairs.
Trail surface:	99% smooth dirt, 1% paved
Sun exposure:	0%
Runability:	100%
Season:	Year-round
Other users:	Hikers, equestrians

Enjoying a weekend run
at Tryon Creek State Park

Canine compatibility:	Leashed dogs permitted
Permits/fees:	None
Trail contact:	Oregon State Parks and Recreation, Salem, OR, (503) 636–9886 or (800) 551–6949, www.oregonstateparks.org/park_144.php
Maps:	USGS Lake Oswego (7.5' series); Tryon Creek State Park trail map, available in the Nature Center or online at www.oregonstateparks.org/park_144.php. The Nature Center is open from 9:00 A.M. to 5:00 P.M. Monday through Friday, and 9:00 A.M. to 4:00 P.M. Saturday and Sunday.

Trail scoop: This 645-acre state park is a forested gem that features more than 14 miles of interconnecting trails designed for runners, hikers, and equestrians. Picturesque Tryon Creek wanders through the heart of this park. Many singletrack trails follow the course of the creek and take you over rolling terrain past immense red cedar, Douglas fir, and big-leaf maple trees. The route described here is only one of dozens you can try. After your run you can learn more about the park's plants and animals at the Nature Center. Rest rooms and water are available at the trailhead.

Finding the trailhead: Take exit 297 off I–5 in Portland and turn south onto Southwest Terwilliger Boulevard. Continue on Southwest Terwilliger Boulevard for 2.7 miles, following signs to Lewis and Clark College and Tryon Creek State Park. Turn right at the Tryon Creek State Park entrance sign. Proceed 0.2 mile on the entrance road to the parking area adjacent to the Nature Center. *DeLorme: Oregon Atlas & Gazetteer:* Page 60 A3.

TRAIL DIRT

0.0 Start on the paved path marked Trillium Trail located on the left side of the Nature Center. Run 50 feet and then head south on the signed Old Main Trail.

0.1 Veer left onto the Old Main Trail (Big Fir Trail heads right.)

0.2 Turn left onto the signed Red Fox Trail.

0.4 Cross Red Fox Bridge over Tryon Creek and begin powering up sweeping switchbacks out of the creek canyon. (Salmonberries and red raspberries provide a sweet treat in midsummer.) At the next trail junction, stay to the right on the Red Fox Trail. At the next trail junction, turn right onto the signed Cedar Trail.

0.8 Turn right and continue on Cedar Trail. (Hemlock Trail goes left.)

0.9 Cross Bunk Bridge over rambling Tryon Creek.

1.2 Continue straight on the Cedar Trail.

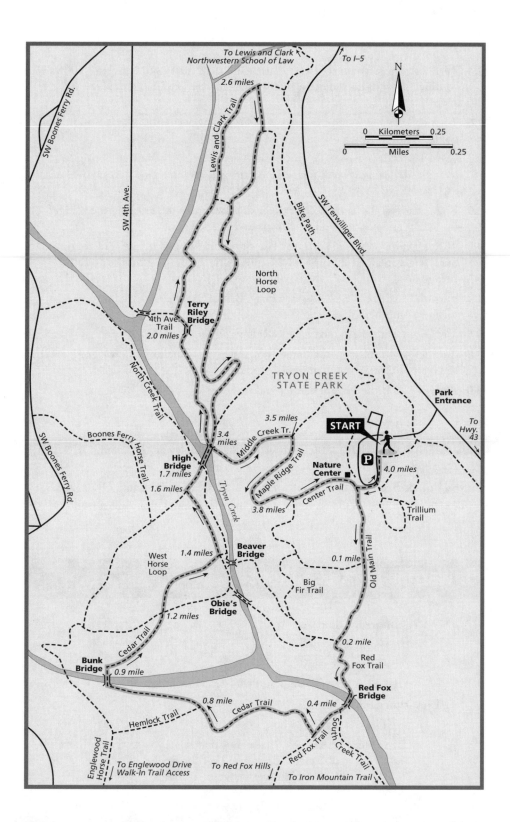

1.4 Turn left where a sign states WEST HORSE LOOP/HIGH BRIDGE. After 100 yards continue straight on the main trail. *(Ignore the unsigned dirt trail that heads right.)*

1.6 Turn right where a sign indicates WEST HORSE LOOP/HIGH BRIDGE. (The trail going left heads toward Boones Ferry Road/Englewood Drive.)

1.7 Cross High Bridge over Tryon Creek. After crossing the bridge, continue straight. At the next trail intersection, turn left where a sign states LEWIS AND CLARK HIKING TRAIL/LAW SCHOOL.

2.0 Bounce across the Terry Riley Suspension Bridge. After crossing the bridge turn right and continue on the Lewis and Clark Trail.

2.6 Turn right on an unsigned trail. (The signed Lewis and Clark Trail continues to the left.) Run about 20 yards to a T intersection. Turn right toward High Bridge.

3.4 Turn right where a sign indicates High Bridge. At the next trail intersection, turn left onto Middle Creek Trail.

3.5 Turn right onto the signed Maple Ridge Trail.

3.8 Turn left onto the signed Center Trail. After this junction follow signs back to the Nature Center and your starting point.

4.0 Arrive back at the Nature Center and trailhead.

TRAIL FOOD

Caro Amico Italian Café, 3606 Southwest Barbur Boulevard, Portland, OR 97201, (503) 223–6895

Fulton Pub & Brewery, 0618 Southwest Nebraska Street, Portland, OR 97201-3556, (503) 246–9530, www.mcmenamins.com/Pubs/Fulton/index.html

9: Warrior Rock Lighthouse

Region/area:	Portland
Pain:	1
Gain:	3
Distance:	6 miles out and back
Elevation gain:	None
Time:	1 to 1.25 hours
The route:	A smooth, shady trail that takes you to the northern tip of Sauvie Island and Warrior Rock Lighthouse. Columbia River views.

Warrior Rock Lighthouse on the Columbia River

Trail surface:	98% smooth dirt, 2% sandy
Sun exposure:	10%
Runability:	100%
Season:	Year-round (can be muddy during the winter months)
Other users:	Hikers
Canine compatibility:	Leashed dogs permitted
Permits/fees:	$3.50 permit required. Permits can be purchased at Sam's Cracker Barrel Store and Reeder Beach RV Park and Store. Sam's Cracker Barrel Store is on the left after crossing the Sauvie Island Bridge. The Reeder Beach RV Park and Store is located on the right after traveling 6.6 miles on Northwest Reeder Road.
Trail contact:	Oregon Department of Fish and Wildlife, Sauvie Island Wildlife Area, Portland, OR, (503) 621–3488, www.dfw.state.or.us/ODFWhtml/InfoCntrWild/WildlifeAreas/Sauvie.html
Map:	USGS St. Helens (7.5' series)

Trail scoop: Escape from the city to enjoy the solitude of this island run. The route travels through a thick cottonwood forest to the northern tip of Sauvie Island along the sandy shores of the Columbia River. Large freighters, tugs, and other ships can be seen sailing up the Columbia to the port of Portland. Wildlife abounds, from great blue herons to bald eagles, not to mention some of the bovine species. At your

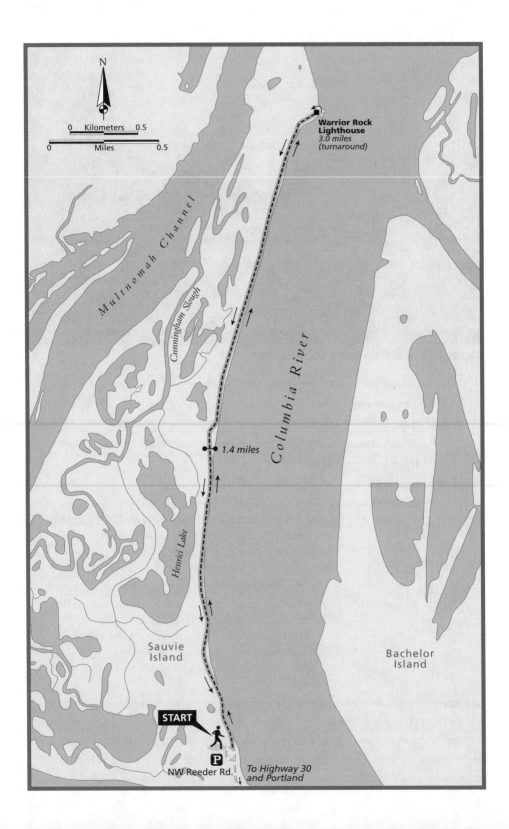

N

0   Kilometers   0.5
0   Miles   0.5

Multnomah Channel

Cunningham Slough

Warrior Rock
Lighthouse
*3.0 miles
(turnaround)*

Columbia River

1.4 miles

Henrici Lake

Sauvie
Island

Bachelor
Island

START

P
NW Reeder Rd.

*To Highway 30
and Portland*

halfway point you can view the white-washed beacon of Warrior Rock Lighthouse, which rests on a sandy beach at the tip of the island. If you run this trail in the fall, golden leaves line the trail with their end-of-the-season brilliance. No water or rest rooms at the trailhead.

Finding the trailhead: From I–405 in Portland, take the Highway 30 West–St. Helens exit and follow the signs for St. Helens. Travel 9.3 miles north on Highway 30 until you see a sign that reads SAUVIE ISLAND WILDLIFE AREA. Exit to the right and cross the bridge to the island. After crossing the bridge continue straight (north) on Northwest Sauvie Island Road for 2.3 miles. Turn right onto Northwest Reeder Road and go 13.2 miles until it dead-ends at a gravel parking area (the last 2.2 miles of this road are gravel). *DeLorme: Oregon Atlas & Gazetteer:* Page 66 B2.

TRAIL DIRT

0.0 Start running north on the singletrack trail located next to a wood trail sign adjacent to the parking area. *(This section of the route can be a bit wild and overgrown.)*

0.4 Step over a low wire fence. (As you continue cruising down this smooth country lane, keep your eye out for juicy blackberries that begin to ripen in mid-to-late August.)

0.5 Turn right on a smooth doubletrack road that continues north through a shady cottonwood forest. Proceed 100 yards and stay to the right at the road junction.

1.4 Go through a blue metal gate. *(Be sure to close the gate or you may let some wily cows out of their pasture.)*

2.8 Turn right on the doubletrack road toward the beach.

3.0 Arrive at a long sandy beach. Soak in the views of the expansive Columbia River and white-washed lighthouse; turn around and head back on the same route.

6.0 Arrive at the trailhead.

TRAIL FOOD

Bridgeport Brewpub, 1313 Northwest Marshall Street, Portland, OR 97209, (503) 241–3612, bridgeportbrew.com/pubs/brewpub.html

Portland Brewing Company, 2730 Northwest 31st Avenue, Portland, OR 97210, (503) 226–7623, www.portlandbrew.com

10: Banks-Vernonia State Trail

Region/area:	Portland
Pain:	1
Gain:	1
Distance:	4 miles out and back (with longer options)
Elevation gain:	210 feet
Time:	30 to 40 minutes
The route:	A wide gravel multiuse trail that travels through a second-growth Douglas fir forest.
Trail surface:	90% gravel, 10% paved
Sun exposure:	5%
Runability:	100%
Season:	Year-round (the trail can be muddy during the winter months)
Other users:	Hikers, mountain bikers, equestrians
Canine compatibility:	Leashed dogs permitted
Permits/fees:	None
Trail contact:	Oregon State Parks and Recreation, Salem, OR, (503) 324–0606 or (800) 551–6949, www.oregonstateparks.org/park_145.php
Maps:	USGS Buxton (7.5' series); *Banks–Vernonia State Trail Guide,* available from Oregon State Parks and Recreation, (800) 551–6949, www.oregonstateparks.org/park_145.php

Trail scoop: You'll enjoy the smooth graded surface on this 20-mile multiuse trail that travels through a serene forest canopy. The route described here is a 4-mile out-and-back section of this trail. However, from the Buxton Trailhead you have the option of heading 14 miles north or 6 miles south as the trail follows the old rail line. This easy track gives you the freedom to go on a slow afternoon ramble or an ambitious marathon. You'll share the trail with mountain bikers, equestrians, and hikers—but more than likely you'll have the trail all to yourself. Rest rooms are available at the trailhead (no water).

Finding the trailhead: From I–405 in Portland head west on U.S. Highway 26, following signs for Beaverton–Ocean Beaches. After approximately 28 miles turn right onto Fisher Road. Go 0.7 mile, passing through the small town of Buxton. Turn right onto Bacona Road and proceed 0.7 mile to the entrance road to the Buxton

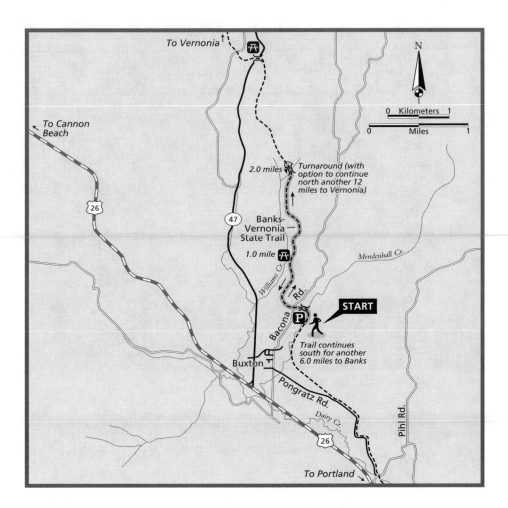

Trailhead, marked by a state park sign. Turn right and go another 0.1 mile to a large parking area and trailhead. *DeLorme: Oregon Atlas & Gazetteer:* Page 65 C7.

TRAIL DIRT

0.0 From the parking area start running north on the paved trail as it heads up a slight incline.

0.1 Cross Bacona Road and continue straight on the gravel trail as it sweeps through a shady forest of Douglas fir, red alder, and sword fern.

2.0 You'll see an interpretive sign on your left perched above a large ravine in an open sunny area. One hundred yards past this sign is a picnic table on the left and your turnaround point. From here, retrace the same route back to the trailhead. (**Option:** Continue north for another 12 miles to the end of the trail in Vernonia, giving you a 28-mile round-trip journey from the trailhead.)

4.0 Arrive back at the trailhead.

Along the Banks-Vernonia State Trail

According to a March 2001 survey sponsored by the All-American Trail Running Association (www.trailrunner.com), the average profile for a trail runner is:

· Average age of men: 37
· Average age of women: 35
· Men: 79.61%
· Women: 20.39%
· Average miles run per week: 25
· Average number of years running trails: 6.4

TRAIL FOOD

Cornelius Pass Roadhouse and Brewery, 4045 Northwest Cornelius Pass Road, Portland, OR 97124, (503) 640–6174, www.mcmenamins.com/Pubs/CPR/index.html

Helvetia Tavern, 10275 Northwest Helvetia Road, Hillsboro, OR 97124, (503) 647–5286

11: Hagg Lake Loop

Region/area:	Portland
Pain:	4
Gain:	3
Distance:	15.1-mile loop
Elevation gain:	100 feet
Time:	2.5 to 3 hours
The route:	Combination of singletrack trail, paved paths, and roads that take you around scenic Hagg Lake in Scoggins Valley Regional Park in Washington County. Bridge crossings.
Trail surface:	20% paved, 75% smooth dirt, 5% rocky
Sun exposure:	40%
Runability:	100%
Season:	April through November
Other users:	Hikers, mountain bikers
Canine compatibility:	Leashed dogs permitted
Permits/fees:	$4.00 day-use fee
Trail contact:	Washington County Parks, Facilities Management Division, Support Services Department, Hillsboro, OR, (503) 846–3692, www.co.washington.or.us/deptmts/ sup_serv/fac_mgt/parks/hagglake.htm
Map:	USGS Gaston and Gales Creek (7.5' series)

Trail scoop: This sinewy trail offers plenty of opportunities for fun as it circles Hagg Lake. The mostly singletrack route weaves in and out of oak woodlands and fir forest and offers plenty of rolling hills. Great swimming holes and juicy blackberries (ripe in mid-August) are some of the many distractions awaiting you. Watch out for mountain bikers blazing this burly route. If you want to compete in a trail-running race around the lake, check out the Hagg Lake Trail Run held in February. Rest rooms are available at the trailhead (no water).

Finding the trailhead: From Portland, head 21 miles west on U.S. Highway 26 to an intersection with Highway 6. Turn left onto Highway 6 (toward Banks, Forest Grove, and Tillamook) and go 2.5 miles to the intersection with Highway 47. Turn south and proceed 12.5 miles to the junction with Scoggins Valley Road. Turn right (west) onto Scoggins Valley Road and head 3.1 miles to the Henry Hagg Lake/Scoggins Valley Park entrance (there is an entrance fee of $4.00 during the

Hagg Lake Trail

summer months). Go 0.3 mile past the entrance booth to the junction with West Shore Drive. Turn left onto West Shore Drive and travel 0.9 mile to a gravel parking area with rest rooms (no water) on the right side of the road. *DeLorme: Oregon Atlas & Gazetteer:* Page 59 A7.

TRAIL DIRT

0.0 From the gravel parking area, turn right (west) and run on the shoulder of West Shore Drive.

0.2 Begin running on the signed singletrack trail on the right side of the road.

0.4 Continue on the main trail to the left.

1.0 Turn left.

1.1 Continue straight at a four-way intersection.

2.0 Continue straight (right). Jog another 20 feet and stay to the left.

2.2 A trail joins the main trail from the left. Stay to the right.

3.3 Turn right where the trail intersects with West Shore Drive and run along the road shoulder.

3.4 Turn right onto the signed singletrack trail.

3.5 The singletrack trail joins a doubletrack dirt road. Jog another 200 feet and arrive at a T intersection with a gravel road. Turn right. (The trail quickly turns back into singletrack.)

3.6 The trail turns into a paved path and takes you through the Sain Creek Picnic

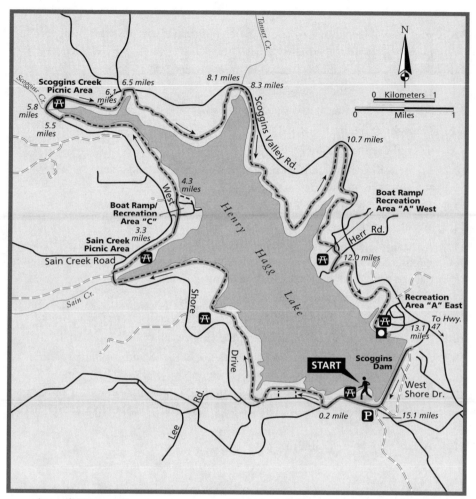

Area. (Water and rest rooms are available here.) Continue running through the picnic area on the paved path past an extravagant pavilion and continue on the signed singletrack trail.

4.0 Arrive at the paved parking area of Boat Ramp/Recreation Area "C". Run through the long parking lot that parallels the lake and pick up the singletrack trail at the other side of the parking area.

4.7 Turn left at a T intersection. Run ahead another 100 feet and then take a right and continue cruising on the singletrack trail.

5.0 Turn right and head downhill.

5.5 Continue straight (left). Go uphill to a paved road. Turn right at the paved road and run on the shoulder.

5.8 Pass the Scoggins Creek Picnic Area on your right. (There are portable toilets but no water at this picnic area.)

6.1 Arrive at a gravel parking area on your right. Pick up the signed singletrack trail at the far end of this parking lot.

6.5 Cross a small bridge and then take a quick right. (If you miss this turn, you'll end up at the paved road.)

6.6 Arrive at a T intersection. Turn right onto a wider trail.

8.1 Arrive at a paved road. Turn right.

8.3 Start running on the signed singletrack trail.

8.7 Turn right at the trail fork.

9.1 Turn right at the trail fork.

10.7 Arrive at the paved road. Turn right on the gravel shoulder and jog 100 feet and continue on the singletrack trail.

11.0 Turn left at the signed trail marker. *(This trail sign is easy to miss!)*

11.2 Turn left at the trail junction.

11.9 Arrive at Boat Ramp/Recreation Area "A" West. (This recreation area has rest rooms and water.) Run across the parking lot and begin heading up the hill on the exit road; look for a trail sign on your right.

12.1 Turn left at the T intersection.

12.5 Continue straight across a faint trail intersection and start powering uphill.

12.8 Turn right and continue running on the singletrack trail.

13.1 Arrive at a paved road. Turn left onto the paved road and continue running until you reach the intersection with Scoggins Valley Road.

13.3 Turn right onto Scoggins Valley Road and run 200 feet on the road shoulder; then turn right onto West Shore Drive. Jog on the road shoulder across the dam.

15.1 Arrive back at the trailhead.

TRAIL FOOD

The Yardhouse Pub at The Grand Lodge, 3505 Pacific Avenue, Forest Grove, OR 97116, (503) 992–3442, www.mcmenamins.com/grandlodge

12: Oaks Bottom Wildlife Refuge

Region/area:	Portland
Pain:	1
Gain:	2
Distance:	3.6 miles out and back
Elevation gain:	30 feet
Time:	30 to 45 minutes

Local spectators at Oaks Bottom Wildlife Refuge

The route:	This dirt path begins at Sellwood Park in Southeast Portland and travels north through Oaks Bottom Wildlife Refuge to the Milwaukee Street Trailhead. Bridge crossings. Willamette River views.
Trail surface:	80% smooth, 20% rocky
Sun exposure:	10%
Runability:	100%
Season:	Year-round
Other users:	Hikers
Canine compatibility:	Leashed dogs permitted
Permits/fees:	None
Trail contact:	Portland Parks & Recreation, Portland, OR, (503) 823–PLAY, www.parks.ci.portland.or.us/Parks/OaksBttmWildRef.htm
Map:	USGS Lake Oswego (7.5' series)

Trail scoop: This out-and-back route passes through the expanse of Oaks Bottom Wildlife Refuge in Southeast Portland. On this run you'll need to adjust your pace so you can get an eyeful of wildlife that abounds in this riparian ecosystem. Great blue herons, Canadian geese, and mallard ducks fly the friendly skies over this Willamette River marsh; while the ground crew of beaver, muskrat, and nutria navigate the waterways. Black cottonwood, dogwood, and elderberry provide shade

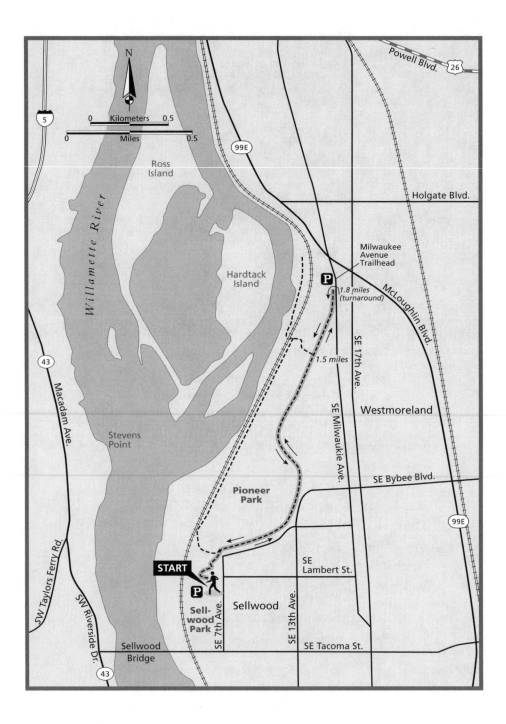

N

![Compass]

5

0   Kilometers   0.5

0   Miles   0.5

Powell Blvd.   26

99E

Holgate Blvd.

Ross
Island

Willamette River

Milwaukee
Avenue
Trailhead

P

1.8 miles
(turnaround)

Hardtack
Island

McLoughlin Blvd.

1.5 miles

SE 17th Ave.

43

Westmoreland

Macadam Ave.

SE Milwaukie Ave.

Stevens
Point

SE Bybee Blvd.

99E

Pioneer
Park

START

SE
Lambert St.

SW Taylors Ferry Rd.

SW Riverside Dr.

P

Sell-
wood
Park

SE 7th Ave.

Sellwood

SE 13th Ave.

Sellwood
Bridge

43

SE Tacoma St.

while you run, and huge thickets of blackberries provide a tasty treat starting in mid-to-late August.

Finding the trailhead: Take exit 297 off I–5 south in Portland and turn south onto Southwest Terwilliger Boulevard. Drive 0.9 mile to the intersection with Southwest Taylors Ferry Road. Turn left onto Southwest Taylors Ferry Road and continue 1.0 mile to the intersection with Macadam Avenue (Highway 43). Turn right (south) onto Highway 43 and go 0.5 mile to the Sellwood Bridge. Head east across the Sellwood Bridge. After crossing the bridge turn left onto Southeast 7th Avenue. Continue approximately 0.5 mile to the parking lot on the left side of the road at Sellwood Park. *DeLorme: Oregon Atlas & Gazetteer:* Page 60 A3.

TRAIL DIRT

0.0 Start running on the dirt path that starts next to the Oaks Bottom Trailhead sign. Head down a series of switchbacks past huge thickets of blackberries that ripen in mid-to-late August.

0.3 Turn right at an unsigned T intersection. Continue running next to the swampy marsh of Oaks Bottom through a canopy of black cottonwood, dogwood, and elderberry trees. (Be on the lookout for Canadian geese, mallard ducks, and blue herons that feed in the reeds and rushes of the marsh.)

1.5 Arrive at a trail intersection located in an open grassy meadow scattered with small trees. Turn right and run up a wide, graveled path to the Milwaukie Avenue Trailhead.

1.8 Arrive at the Milwaukie Avenue Trailhead. From this trailhead retrace your route back to your starting point at Sellwood Park.

3.6 Arrive at the trailhead.

TRAIL FOOD

Ironhorse Mexican Restaurant, 6034 Southeast Milwaukie Avenue, Portland, OR 97202, (503) 232–1826

Gino's Restaurant and Bar, 8057 Southeast 13th Avenue, Portland, OR 97202, (503) 233–4613

13: Mount Tabor Loop

Region/area:	Portland
Pain:	2
Gain:	3
Distance:	1.7-mile loop
Elevation gain:	250 feet
Time:	20 to 30 minutes
The route:	Nice singletrack route that circles Mount Tabor through a shady Douglas fir forest. Short sections of paved road and paved pedestrian path. City and mountain views.
Trail surface:	90% smooth dirt, 10% paved
Sun exposure:	20%
Runability:	100%
Season:	Year-round
Other users:	Hikers, mountain bikers
Canine compatibility:	Leashed dogs permitted
Permits/fees:	None
Trail contact:	Portland Parks & Recreation, Portland, OR, (503) 823–PLAY, www.parks.ci.portland.or.us/Parks/MtTabor.htm
Map:	USGS Mount Tabor (7.5' series)

Finding the trailhead: From downtown Portland head 5.5 miles east on I–84 toward The Dalles. Exit the freeway at 82nd Avenue (exit 5). At the end of the off-ramp and stop sign, turn right and go 1 block to a stoplight at the intersection with Northeast 82nd Avenue. Turn left (south) onto Northeast 82nd Avenue and travel 1.1 miles to the intersection with Southeast Yamhill Street. Turn right onto Southeast Yamhill Street and proceed 0.3 mile west to the intersection with Southeast 76th Street. Turn right on Southeast 76th Street and then take an immediate left onto Southeast Yamhill Street and continue heading west for 0.3 mile to the intersection with Southeast 69th Street. Turn left onto Southeast 69th Street, go 1 block, and turn right onto an unmarked paved road at the base of Mount Tabor Park. Continue 0.2 mile to a parking area on the right side of the road. *DeLorme: Oregon Atlas & Gazetteer:* Page 66 D4.

Trail scoop: Mount Tabor Park is one of those urban sanctuaries where you can still find wild in the city. This prominent volcanic butte rises above Portland's skyline bursting with urban greenery. Where else can you run to the top of a three-million-

City views from Mount Tabor Park

year-old volcano covered with a Douglas fir and conifer forest? This 200-acre park is crisscrossed with sweet dirt trails that are a trail runner's dream, and the views of Portland's east side from the 643-foot summit are stellar. You can follow the route cues for this fun loop route or you can create your own route. This park is well loved and during the peak summer months, bikers, hikers, kids, and dogs abound. Rest rooms and water are available at the parking area.

TRAIL DIRT

0.0 Start running on the dirt path that starts in the northeast corner of the parking area next to the rest rooms. After a short jaunt you'll arrive at a trail junction. Turn right and run past big ol' Douglas fir trees along the west side of Mount Tabor.

0.3 Cross a gravel road and continue straight on the dirt path.

0.4 Arrive at a four-way junction. Continue straight on the singletrack trail. Go 25 yards and arrive at a T junction. Go right and continue on the singletrack trail.

0.5 Cross a paved park entrance road and continue straight on the singletrack trail on a fun descent. Go 50 yards and take a sharp left at the drinking fountain and run parallel to the tennis courts. (The tennis courts are on your right.)

0.6 Arrive at a trail junction. Stay to the left and pounce uphill. (You are now above the reservoir.) (**Sidetrip:** If you want some extra mileage, you can jog around the reservoir on the paved path.) At the next trail junction, cross a paved path and stairs and continue straight for 20 feet to a trail fork. Turn left.

0.7 Turn right at the trail fork.

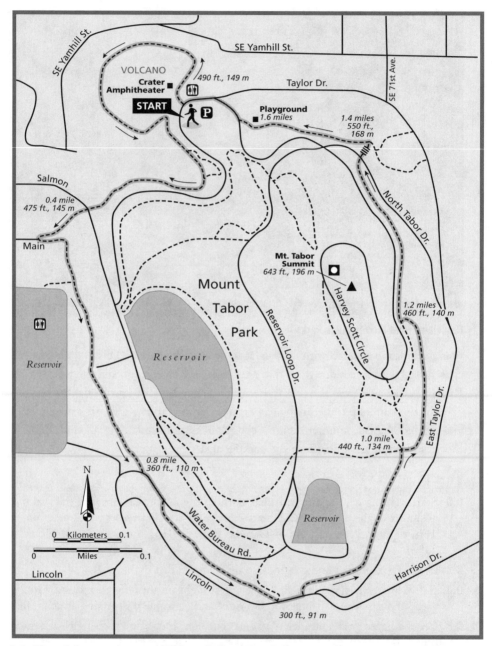

0.8 Turn left onto the paved Water Bureau Road. Continue 50 yards uphill on the road shoulder and then peel right onto a dirt path. (Ignore spur trails that head left.)

0.9 Turn right onto a dirt path and go about 35 yards. Turn left onto a paved road. Run about 50 yards along the road shoulder and then swing a left onto a dirt path. Go 15 yards to a T intersection. Turn right and crank uphill. At the next trail junction, turn right and continue motoring up the steep grade. (Ignore spur trails that head left.)

1.0 Arrive at a five-way junction. Turn right and continue running on the wide dirt path as it goes around the east side of Mount Tabor. (**Sidetrip:** If you go straight the path takes you to the summit of Mount Tabor.)

1.2 Turn right at the T intersection and continue sailing on the smooth singletrack trail.

1.4 Cross North Tabor Drive and run down a flight of steps. Take a sharp left onto a singletrack trail.

1.6 The trail turns to concrete and passes through a little kiddy playground. Jog on the concrete path through the playground until it intersects with a paved road. (Look for a drinking fountain on your right before this junction.) Cross the paved road. After crossing the road turn right and run downhill on the sidewalk.

1.7 Turn left onto the paved road and then take an immediate right into the parking area and your starting point.

TRAIL FOOD

Ya Hala Lebanese Cuisine, 8005 Southeast Stark Street, Portland, OR 97215, (503) 256–4484

14: Powell Butte Nature Park Loop

Region/area:	Portland
Pain:	2
Gain:	2
Distance:	3.5-mile loop
Elevation gain:	300 feet
Time:	25 to 40 minutes
The route:	This route takes you through open meadowlands and thick forest in Powell Butte Nature Park in Southeast Portland. City and mountain views.
Trail surface:	85% dirt, 15% paved
Sun exposure:	35%
Runability:	100%
Season:	Year-round
Other users:	Hikers, mountain bikers, equestrians

A quiet city escape at Powell Butte Nature Park

Canine compatibility:	Leashed dogs permitted
Permits/fees:	None
Trail contact:	Portland Parks & Recreation, Portland, OR, (503) 823–PLAY, www.parks.ci.portland.or.us
Maps:	USGS Gladstone and Damascus (7.5' series); Powell Butte Nature Park trail map, available at the trailhead or by calling Portland Parks and Recreation, (503) 823–PLAY

Trail scoop: Powell Butte Nature Park is located on an extinct volcano that features diverse habitats and wildlife. This 570-acre park is riddled with a system of interconnecting trails that wind through open grassy meadows, old fruit orchards, and thick woodlands made up of western red cedar, Douglas fir, alder, and big-leaf maple trees. This fast-and-furious loop trail gives you a taste for the excellent trails this park has to offer. If you're feeling spunky after completing the loop, go hog wild and do it again, or come up with your own route. Rest rooms and water are available at the trailhead.

Finding the trailhead: From I–205 in southeast Portland head east on Southeast Division Street. Go 3.5 miles and turn right onto Southeast 162nd Avenue. Continue 0.7 mile to the entrance of Powell Butte Nature Park. Proceed 0.3 mile to a large parking area and the trailhead. *DeLorme: Oregon Atlas & Gazetteer:* Page 60 A4.

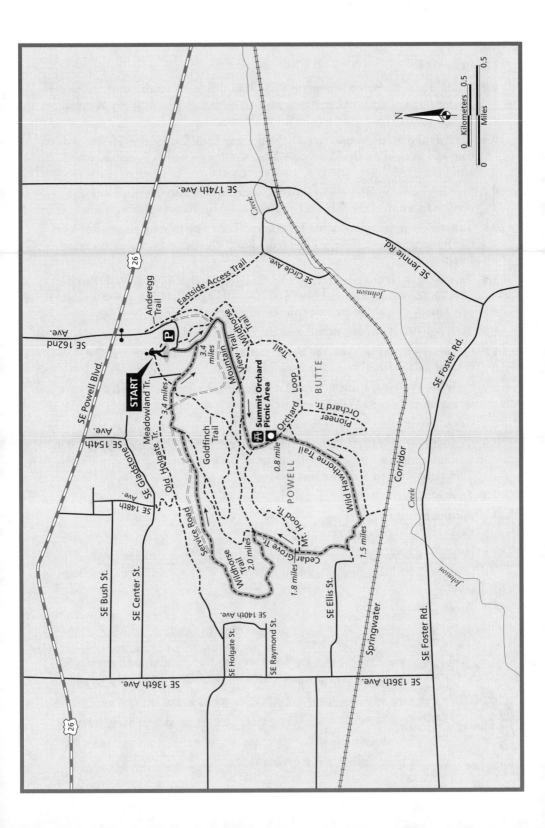

TRAIL DIRT

0.0 Warm up on the paved Mountain View Trail that starts on the west end of the concrete patio next to the rest rooms. (This wide path gradually heads uphill along a grassy hillside scattered with wildflowers.)

0.6 Turn right onto the singletrack Orchard Loop Trail. Go another 20 feet and continue straight on the Wildhorse Trail. Continue another 50 feet and turn left.

0.7 Veer left onto the Orchard Loop Trail, which winds through an open meadow scattered with thickets of black hawthorn and Himalayan blackberry trees.

0.8 Turn right on the signed Wild Hawthorne Trail. The turn for this trail is located 50 feet past the trail sign. (The route heads on a long downhill into a cool forest.)

1.5 Turn right at an unsigned dirt intersection. Jog another 100 feet and then peel right on the signed Mount Hood Trail. (You'll begin climbing as the trail winds past fern-covered hills and towering fir and red cedar trees.)

1.6 Turn right and continue running on the Mount Hood Trail.

1.8 Continue straight (left) on the signed Cedar Grove Trail. Enjoy this fast descent as it swishes through a maze of green.

2.0 Turn left and cross a small creek. After crossing the creek, head left and start loping on the signed Wildhorse Trail.

2.5 Continue straight (right). (Ignore the path that drops off steeply on your left.)

2.6 Continue straight (left). (Ignore the trail on the right that heads steeply uphill.) Continue another 30 feet past this intersection and arrive at a crest in the trail. Turn right onto an unsigned dirt trail.

2.8 Turn left onto an unsigned dirt trail.

3.0 Turn right onto a gravel road.

3.2 Veer right at the signed Meadowland Trail.

3.4 Continue straight on the Meadowland Trail. After about 200 feet head left on a singletrack trail that heads downhill toward the rest rooms and your starting point.

3.5 Arrive at the trailhead.

The First Trail Race?

It is thought that the first trail race happened in Scotland around 1068. The race was held in the small town of Braemar (located about 75 miles north of Edinburgh) and it was to the top of a formidable 1,764-foot hill called Creag Choinnich. The winning time was achieved in about three minutes, with the winner receiving a small amount of gold, a sword, and a decorated belt.

TRAIL FOOD

Campbell's Bar-B-Q, 8701 Southeast Powell Boulevard, Portland, OR 97266, (503) 777–9795

15: Glendoveer Fitness Trail Loop

Region/area:	Portland
Pain:	1
Gain:	2
Distance:	2-mile loop
Elevation gain:	40 feet
Time:	15 to 30 minutes
The Route:	Wood-chip trail (with a short paved section) that circles Glendoveer Golf Course in northeast Portland.
Trail surface:	Wood chips 70%, dirt 20%, paved 10%
Sun exposure:	70%
Runability:	100%
Season:	Year-round
Other users:	Walkers
Canine compatibility:	Dogs are not permitted
Permits/fees:	None
Trail contact:	Metro Regional Parks and Greenspaces, Portland, OR, (503) 797–1850, www.metroregion.org/parks/glendoveer.html
Map:	USGS Mount Tabor (7.5' series)

Finding the trailhead: From I–205 south in Portland, take the Stark Street exit. Continue on the off-ramp to the junction with Northeast Glisan Street. Turn left (east) onto Northeast Glisan Street and go 2.8 miles to the intersection with Northeast 148th Avenue. Turn left onto Northeast 148th Avenue and continue 0.5 mile to a parking area on the left side of the road at the Glendoveer Golf Course. (The parking area is right before the intersection with Northeast Halsey Street.)

From I–205 north in Portland, take the Glisan Street exit. Turn right (east) onto Northeast Glisan Street and go 2.8 miles to the intersection with Northeast 148th Avenue. Turn left onto Northeast 148th Avenue and continue 0.5 mile to a parking area on the left side of the road at the Glendoveer Golf Course. (The parking

Glendoveer Fitness Trail

area is right before the intersection with Northeast Halsey Street.) *DeLorme: Oregon Atlas & Gazetteer:* Page 66 D4.

Trail scoop: This sophisticated wood-chip trail circles the smooth greens of Glendoveer Golf Course in northeast Portland. A short hill will make you catch your breath at the start but after that it's smooth sailing. Water and rest rooms are available at the trailhead.

TRAIL DIRT

0.0 Start running clockwise on the soft and bouncy wood-chip trail as it heads up a short hill and parallels Northeast 148th Avenue. (The trail enters a shady Douglas fir forest that is a welcome relief on a hot summer's day. You may have to dodge other runners and walkers, who flock to this popular urban trail.)

0.5 The trail turns west and parallels Northeast Glisan Street. (There is a chain-link fence on both sides of the trail.)

0.8 The wood-chip trail ends; exit to the left onto the sidewalk. Begin running on the sidewalk as it parallels Northeast Glisan Street. Continue running on the sidewalk past the Glendoveer Tennis Center and the Ringside Restaurant and Lounge on your right.

1.0 Turn right on the wood-chip trail just to the right of the chain-link fence. The path quickly turns to pavement. Run 50 yards and stay to the right at the trail fork. After another 30 feet stay to the right again and continue running on the paved path.

1.1 The paved path ends and turns into a dirt path.

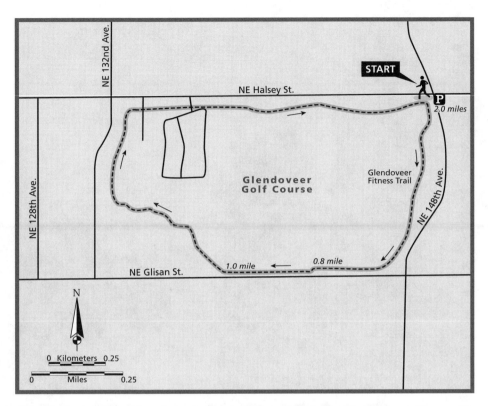

1.2 Cross a paved path and continue straight on the wood-chip fitness trail.

2.0 Arrive back at the trailhead. If you're feeling energetic go for another round.

TRAIL FOOD

McMenamins Pub 205, 9710 Southeast Washington Street, Suite A, Portland OR
97216, (503) 254–5411, www.mcmenamins.com/Pubs/Mc205/index.html

Ringside Steakhouse, 14021 Northeast Glisan Street, Portland, OR 97230, (503)
255–0750

16: Clackamas River

Region/area:	Portland
Pain:	3 for the one-way shuttle; 5 for the out-and-back option
Gain:	4
Distance:	8 miles (with a shuttle) or 16 miles out and back
Elevation gain:	300 feet

The Clackamas River

Time:	2 to 2.5 hours (one-way with shuttle) or 4 to 4.5 hours (out and back)
The route:	A classic river trail that traces the contours of the Clackamas River through pockets of old-growth western red cedar and Douglas fir. River views. Creek crossings. Bridge crossings.
Trail surface:	60% smooth dirt, 40% rocky
Sun exposure:	5%
Runability:	100%
Season:	April through November
Other users:	Hikers
Canine compatibility:	Dogs permitted
Permits/fees:	$5.00 Northwest Forest Pass, purchased by calling (800) 270–7504, or online at www.naturenw.org
Trail contact:	Mount Hood National Forest, Estacada Ranger Station, Estacada, OR, (503) 630–8700, www.fs.fed.us/r6/mthood/crtrails.htm
Maps:	USGS Fish Creek Mountain, Three Lynx, Bedford Point (7.5' series); Green Trails Fish Creek Mountain

Trail scoop: This challenging river trail takes you on a mystical journey through pockets of mossy old-growth forest that will astound you. Revel in their greatness but remember to watch your feet because sections of this trail can be very rocky. You'll also enjoy great views of the Clackamas River at several different points where the trail drops down to almost river level. The only blemishes to this fabulous trail are when the route crosses through open areas with power lines. Rest rooms are available at both trailheads (no water).

Finding the trailhead: From I–205 in southeast Portland, take exit 12A for Highway 212/Highway 224/Clackamas/Estacada. Head east for 3.5 miles and then veer right onto Highway 224 toward Estacada. You'll reach Estacada in about 14 more miles. From Estacada, continue 14.7 miles east on Highway 224 to the turnoff for Fish Creek Campground. Turn right onto Fish Creek Road (unsigned) and go 0.3 mile to a large parking area on the right. This is the end (or turnaround point) for the run. If you are doing a shuttle, leave a bike or car at this trailhead.

To continue to the upper trailhead, turn left out of the parking area on Fish Creek Road. Go 0.3 mile. Turn right (east) onto Highway 224 and go 6.6 miles. Turn right onto unsigned Forest Service Road 4620 toward Indian Henry Campground. Travel 0.6 mile on Forest Service Road 4620 and turn right into the trailhead parking area opposite the entrance to Indian Henry Campground. *DeLorme: Oregon Atlas & Gazetteer:* Page 61 D8.

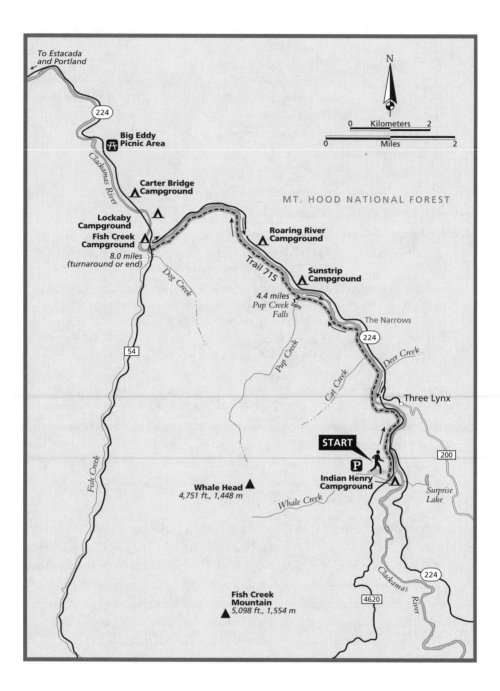

To Estacada
and Portland

224

**Big Eddy
Picnic Area**

Clackamas River

**Carter Bridge
Campground**

MT. HOOD NATIONAL FOREST

**Lockaby
Campground**
**Fish Creek
Campground**
8.0 miles
(turnaround or end)

**Roaring River
Campground**

Trail 715

**Sunstrip
Campground**

4.4 miles
Pup Creek
Falls

The Narrows

224

54

Dog Creek

Pup Creek

Cat Creek

Deer Creek

Three Lynx

200

START

Fish Creek

**Indian Henry
Campground**

Whale Head ▲
4,751 ft., 1,448 m

Whale Creek

Surprise
Lake

Clackamas River

224

**Fish Creek
Mountain**
▲ 5,098 ft., 1,554 m

4620

N

0   Kilometers   2

0   Miles   2

TRAIL DIRT

0.0 Begin running on the singletrack trail at a wood trail sign. Almost immediately you'll need to turn right as the trail passes through a cool mossy forest. (The first 2.9 miles the trail has many fun ups and downs that take you through magnificent old growth. Distractions on the trail include a basalt overhang where you'll have to duck as the trail passes underneath and a small cascading waterfall. The trail continues rolling up and down ridges, giving you a good cardio workout. It also weaves through pockets of old growth and in and out of an old clear-cut area with not-so-pretty power lines where the trail tends to be overgrown. You'll also travel past The Narrows—a narrow basalt gorge where the river rushes through a 20-foot-wide rock channel.)

4.4 Cross Pup Creek over a rock path. (**Sidetrip:** Just after you cross the creek, turn left and jog 200 yards up a side trail to view the feathery cascade of Pup Creek Falls.)

7.3 Pass a tantalizing sandy beach that may tempt you to stop and take a swim on a hot day. (If you are running out and back, remember this spot on your return trip.)

8.0 The trail intersects with Fish Creek Road, your turnaround point. (**Option:** If you are completing a car or bike shuttle, cross Fish Creek Road to the trailhead parking area.) Retrace the same route to your starting point.

16.0 Arrive at the trailhead.

TRAIL FOOD

Deli Delite, 372 North Broadway Street, Estacada, OR 97023, (503) 630–4446

17: Riverside Trail

Region/area:	Portland
Pain:	2
Gain:	4
Distance:	8.4 miles out and back
Elevation gain:	130 feet
Time:	2 to 2.5 hours
The route:	A classic river trail that traces the contours of the Clackamas River through pockets of old-growth western red cedar and Douglas fir. River views. Creek crossings. Bridge crossings.
Trail surface:	65% smooth dirt, 35% rocky

Sage leading the way on the Riverside Trail

Sun exposure:	5%
Runability:	100%
Season:	April through November
Other users:	Hikers, mountain bikers
Canine compatibility:	Dogs permitted
Permits/fees:	$5.00 Northwest Forest Pass, purchased by calling (800) 270–7504, or online at www.naturenw.org
Trail contact:	Mount Hood National Forest, Estacada Ranger Station, Estacada, OR, (503) 630–8700, www.fs.fed.us/r6/mthood/crtrails.htm
Map:	USGS Fish Creek Mountain

Trail scoop: This route offers some of the best river running close to Portland. It is a blend of short, intense uphills and downhills with a fun mix of technical obstacles. Immense red cedars, cool mossy forest, and the soothing sounds of the Clackamas River are the backdrop to this radically fun run. Additional distractions that will keep you grinning include superb swimming holes and stunning viewpoints of the Clackamas River. Water and rest rooms are available in the campground.

Finding the trailhead: From I–205 in southeast Portland, take exit 12A for Highway 212/Highway 224/Clackamas/Estacada. Head east for 3.5 miles and then veer right onto Highway 224 toward Estacada. You'll reach Estacada in about 14 miles. From

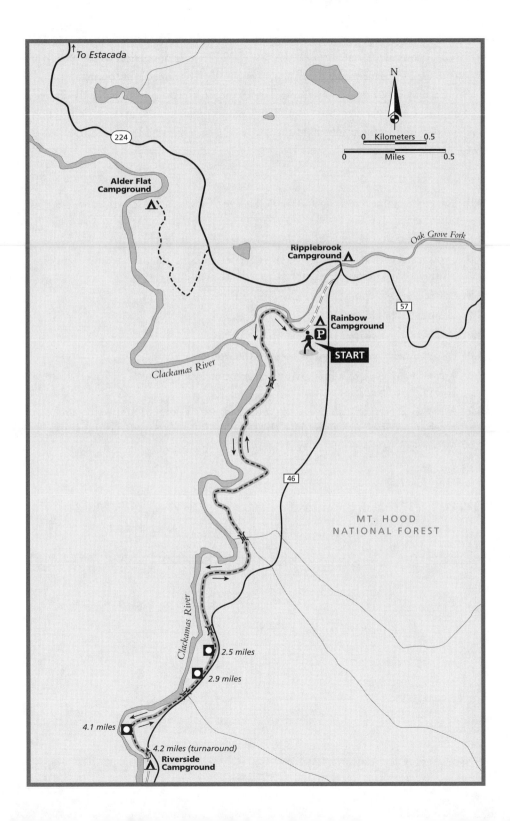

To Estacada

224

Alder Flat
Campground

Oak Grove Fork

Ripplebrook
Campground

57

Rainbow
Campground

P
START

Clackamas River

46

MT. HOOD
NATIONAL FOREST

Clackamas River

2.5 miles

2.9 miles

4.1 miles

4.2 miles (turnaround)

Riverside
Campground

N

0   Kilometers   0.5

0   Miles   0.5

Estacada, continue 25 miles east on Highway 224 to a road junction (right after you cross the Oak Grove Fork of the Clackamas River). Continue right toward Detroit/Bagby Hot Springs on Forest Service Road 46. Almost immediately after making this turn, veer right into Rainbow Campground. Continue 0.3 mile through the campground to the trailhead at the end of the campground loop road. *DeLorme: Oregon Atlas & Gazetteer:* Page 66 D8.

TRAIL DIRT

0.0 Start by heading south on the singletrack trail. Cross a creek with some large boulders.

2.5 Pass a great viewpoint of the Clackamas River on the right.

2.6 Cross a wood bridge over a side creek. After crossing the bridge, turn right and continue cruising on the signed Riverside Trail #723.

2.9 Pass a great viewpoint of the Clackamas River on the right.

3.1 Continue straight (left).

3.6 Pass by a great swimming beach on the right.

4.0 Pass another great swimming hole on the right.

4.1 Arrive at the crest of a hill, giving you a commanding view of the river. From here enjoy a steep, fun descent.

4.2 Arrive at Riverside Campground (your turnaround point). (Rest rooms and water are available here.) Retrace the same route back to your starting point.

8.4 Arrive back at the trailhead at Rainbow Campground.

TRAIL FOOD

Deli Delite, 372 North Broadway Street, Estacada, OR 97023, (503) 630–4446

Columbia River Gorge

The western edge of the Columbia River Gorge is a quick thirty-minute drive east of Portland on I–84. This magnificent river gorge is carved by the mile-wide Columbia River—the dividing line between Oregon and Washington—and has one of the highest concentrations of waterfalls in North America. Thanks to legislation passed in 1986, the Columbia Gorge is a designated national scenic area. This scenic stretch of river canyon is home to hundreds of miles of trails that take you past magical waterfalls and rocky creeks, through deep forest canopy, and to the top of prominent cliffs that offer endless views of the Columbia River and Cascade peaks. Many of the trails in the gorge offer tons of elevation gain, promising an excellent workout. Trails that should not be missed are the Angels Rest, Wahkeenah Falls Loop, Horsetail–Oneonta–Triple Falls, the epic Larch Mountain Trail, and the gorgeous Eagle Creek Trail.

18: Angels Rest

Region/area:	Columbia River Gorge
Pain:	4
Gain:	4
Distance:	4.4 miles out and back
Elevation gain:	1,500 feet
Time:	1 to 1.5 hours
The route:	Singletrack trail that ascends a steep, forested ridge to a spectacular summit in the Columbia River Gorge. Waterfall. Bridge crossing. Summit views.
Trail surface:	55% smooth dirt, 45% rocky
Sun exposure:	40%
Runability:	95%
Season:	Year-round (the trail can be muddy and icy during the winter months)
Other users:	Hikers
Canine compatibility:	Leashed dogs permitted
Permits/fees:	None
Trail contact:	USDA Forest Service, Columbia River Gorge National Scenic Area, Hood River, OR 97031, (541) 386–2333, www.fs.fed.us/r6/columbia/trails/trail_415.htm
Maps:	USGS Bridal Veil (7.5' series); USFS Trails of the Columbia River Gorge; Green Trails Bridal Veil

Trail scoop: This challenging route is a great introduction to the steep and sustained nature of trails in the Columbia River Gorge. It's a perfect late-afternoon getaway from the hectic Portland scene to a tranquil deep forest and open spaces carved by the Columbia River. Your run starts with a mild grade on nice dirt that sweeps through a cool forest canopy. Soon enough the trail throws in a few rocky sections as the grade becomes steeper. Views soon abound as you proceed through a burn area dating from the early 1990s. Pat yourself on the back here if you're still breaking stride as the unrelenting grade continues. Nearing the summit you'll encounter a rather unusual boulder field that is probably best strolled through. Blast out of the final switchback onto the palatial ridge of Angels Rest. For summer outings this trail can be hot and is best experienced early or late and water is a must. No rest rooms or water are available at the trailhead.

Finding the trailhead: From Portland, head 28 miles east on I–84 to Bridal Veil Falls,

A perfect rest stop at the summit of Angels Rest

exit 28. After you exit the freeway, go 0.3 mile and turn right onto the Historic Columbia River Highway. Park your vehicle in the paved trailhead parking lot located on the right side of the road.

If you are coming from the east, take exit 35 off I–84 and travel approximately 7.3 miles west on the Historic Columbia River Highway until you reach the paved trailhead parking area on the right side of the road. *DeLorme: Oregon Atlas & Gazetteer:* Page 67 D7.

TRAIL DIRT

0.0 Start by heading to the west end of the parking lot and crossing the Historic Columbia River Highway. Jog up a short set of stone steps and begin running on the signed dirt path. After approximately 100 yards you'll arrive at a T intersection. Stay to the left and continue on the main trail. (The trail going right heads toward the overflow parking lot.) The path is very rocky and steep as it takes you through a shady fern-filled forest.

0.3 Power up an open, rocky slope with good views of the Columbia River.

0.5 (**Sidetrip:** Stop and take a peek of the sweeping cascade of Coopey Falls from a viewpoint on your left.)

0.6 Cross a wood bridge over tumbling Coopey Creek.

1.4 Enjoy some great gorge views as you ascend through an old burn area.

2.1 (The trail passes through a boulder field that is home to a colony of rabbit-like rodents called pikas. As you bounce over this rocky section, you'll no doubt hear the warning *cheeep cheeep* call made by these cute little critters.)

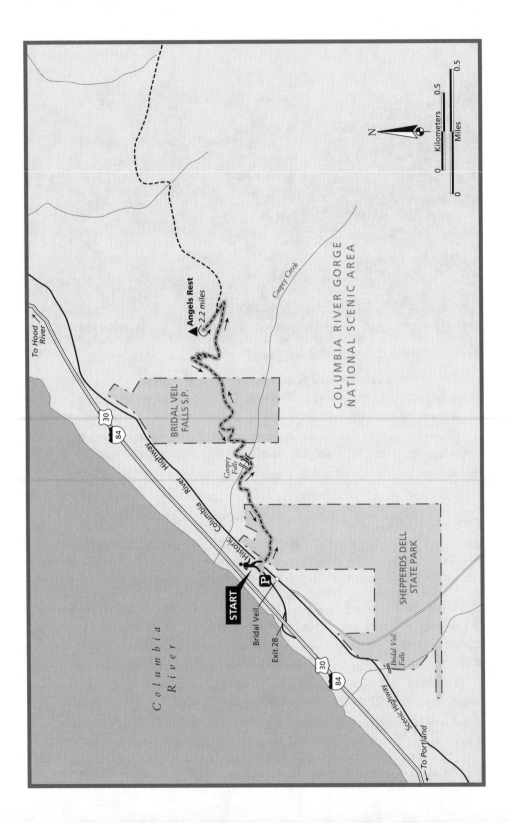

2.2 Turn left, climb up a short set of boulders, and continue until you reach the summit viewpoint. Lounge at the summit, admire the views, and gear up for the descent on the same trail that will take you back to your starting point.

4.4 Arrive at the trailhead.

TRAIL FOOD

Black Rabbit Restaurant at McMenamins Edgefield, 2126 Southwest Halsey Street, Troutdale, OR 97060, (503) 492–3086, www.mcmenamins.com

Multnomah Falls Lodge Restaurant, 50000 Historic Columbia River Highway, Bridal Veil, OR 97010, (503) 695–2376, www.multnomahfallslodge.com

19: Wahkeenah Falls Loop

Region/area:	Columbia River Gorge
Pain:	4
Gain:	5
Distance:	4.9-mile loop
Elevation gain:	1,600 feet
Time:	1.25 to 1.5 hours
The route:	Dirt and paved path that takes you into a green and watery world where you'll have fantastic views of Multnomah Falls, Multnomah Creek, Wahkeenah Creek, Wahkeenah Falls. Bridge crossings. Creek crossings. Columbia River Gorge views.
Trail surface:	55% smooth dirt, 25% rocky, 20% paved
Sun exposure:	10%
Runability:	95%
Season:	Year-round
Other users:	Hikers
Canine compatibility:	Leashed dogs permitted
Permits/fees:	None
Trail contact:	USDA Forest Service, Columbia River Gorge National Scenic Area, Hood River, OR 97031, (541) 386–2333, www.fs.fed.us/r6/columbia
Maps:	USGS Bridal Veil and Multnomah Falls (7.5' series); USFS Trails of the Columbia River Gorge

Wahkeenah Falls in the background

Trail scoop: Welcome to the green and watery world of the Columbia River Gorge! This trail begins at historic Multnomah Falls Lodge and takes you on an uphill odyssey on a paved path to the top of spectacular Multnomah Falls. You'll have to brave crowds gawking at the falls the first mile, but then you'll leave them behind and enter a gorgeous creek canyon filled with waterfalls, rocky outcrops, and fern-covered hillsides. The trail continues on its upward journey as it turns away from Multnomah Creek and winds its way across a ridge through a magnificent fir forest. It then hooks up with Wahkeenah Creek and spirals down a series of switchbacks that skip back and forth across this mossy, bouldery creek. On the way down you'll be mesmerized by the spectacular splashes of Upper and Lower Wahkeenah Falls. You'll finish the loop by hooking up with a short dirt path at the Wahkeenah Falls trailhead that takes you back to your starting point at historic Multnomah Falls Lodge. Rest rooms and water are available at the trailhead.

Finding the trailhead: From the intersection of I–205 and I–84 in Portland, head 21 miles east on I–84 to the Multnomah Falls exit (#31). Park in the large paved parking area. To reach the trailhead, go through the tunnel (under I–84) and follow the broad paved steps, which lead you to the trailhead behind Multnomah Falls Lodge. *DeLorme: Oregon Atlas & Gazetteer:* Page 66 D8.

TRAIL DIRT

0.0 Start running on the paved path next to Multnomah Falls Lodge. (As the trail climbs you'll contend with a series of stairs and hordes of people you'll have to dash by.)

0.1 Pass a sign that indicates MULTNOMAH FALLS BRIDGE 0.2/TOP OF FALLS 1/WAHKEENAH TRAIL 1.8/LARCH MOUNTAIN 6.8.

0.2 Turn (or walk depending how many people are here) across a magnificent bridge that spans Multnomah Creek and has a striking view of Multnomah Falls.

1.0 Arrive at the crest of the hill and then the paved trail begins to descend a short

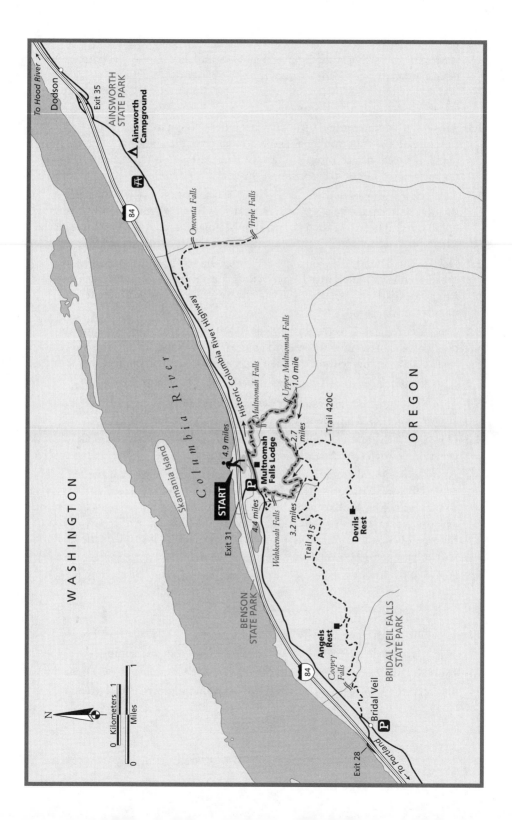

ways until you arrive at a T intersection. Continue left on the dirt path. (The path that heads right leads to an overlook of Multnomah Falls.) Cross a stone bridge over the creek. After you cross the creek the trail starts climbing up the scenic Multnomah Creek Canyon.

1.1 Arrive at a T intersection. Turn left onto Larch Mountain Trail 441. (As you continue on the trail, you'll be tempted to gawk at the amazing waterfalls and bubbling creek instead of watching your feet—this can be hazardous on some of the rocky stretches on this section of the trail.)

1.7 Arrive at a T intersection with a sign that reads WAHKEENAH TRAIL #420/ WAHKEENAH TRAILHEAD 2.7/ANGELS REST 1.2. Turn right and continue your uphill on Wahkeenah Trail #420. (Larch Mountain Trail #441 continues to the left.)

2.7 Devil's Rest Trail #420C joins the trail from the left. Continue straight. Jog ahead another 100 feet to a T intersection. Turn right at the sign VISTA POINT #419/WAHKEENAH 1/COLUMBIA RIVER HIGHWAY 1.9. (**Option:** Go left for a more gradual descent.)

3.2 Cross Wahkeenah Creek and then jog 100 feet to a trail intersection toward COLUMBIA HIGHWAY/WAHKEENAH FALLS TRAILHEAD 1.2. Turn right and continue your steep descent on multiple switchbacks next to Wahkeenah Creek.

3.5 (Pass the gorgeous cascade of Upper Wahkeenah Falls on your right.)

3.7 Turn right and continue your fast descent. (**Option:** If you go left you'll arrive at a viewpoint of the Columbia River Gorge.)

4.2 (The trail turns into a paved path. Proceed another 100 yards and soak in the views of Lower Wahkeenah Falls on your left.)

4.4 Arrive at the Wahkeenah Falls trailhead located at the bottom of the hill next to the Historic Columbia River Highway. Continue on the paved path, cross a wood bridge over Wahkeenah Creek, and then look for the sign RETURN TRAIL TO MULTNOMAH FALLS .5 MILE. (The paved trail ends 200 feet after you cross the wood bridge.) Continue east on the Return Trail as it parallels the Historic Columbia River Highway.

4.9 Arrive at Multnomah Falls Lodge and your starting point.

TRAIL FOOD

Black Rabbit Restaurant at McMenamins Edgefield, 2126 Southwest Halsey Street, Troutdale, OR 97060, (503) 492–3086, www.mcmenamins.com

Multnomah Falls Lodge Restaurant, 50000 Historic Columbia River Highway, Bridal Veil, OR 97010, (503) 695–2376, www.multnomahfallslodge.com

Region/area:	Columbia River Gorge
Pain:	5
Gain:	5
Distance:	13.6 miles out and back
Elevation gain:	3,800 feet
Time:	5 to 7 hours
The route:	A classic Columbia River Gorge run that travels next to magnificent Multnomah Creek and then takes you to the spectacular summit of Larch Mountain. Waterfalls. Bridge crossings. Mountain views.
Trail surface:	50% smooth dirt, 35% rocky, 15% paved
Sun exposure:	10%
Runability:	100%
Season:	Mid-May through October
Other users:	Hikers
Canine compatibility:	Leashed dogs permitted
Permits/fees:	None
Trail contact:	Columbia River Gorge National Scenic Area, Hood River, OR, (541) 386–2333, www.fs.fed.us/r6/columbia
Maps:	USGS Multnomah Falls (7.5' series); Green Trails Bridal Veil; USFS Trails of the Columbia River Gorge

Trail scoop: This adventure starts at Multnomah Falls, one of the most visited attractions in Oregon. The initial mile to the top of the hill is steep, paved, and crowded. On a busy weekend you may as well walk it, lest you confront major people navigation and the ire of folks just barely making it. Take heart, 99.9 percent of the people will turn around at the top of the falls, leaving you with an ethereal dirt trail all to yourself. After you reach the top of the falls, the trail turns to dirt and you'll run next to the pristine waters of Multnomah Creek and then charge up moderate grades to the 4,056-foot summit of Larch Mountain. At the top you'll have superb views of Mount Rainier, Mount St. Helens, Mount Adams, Mount Hood, Mount Jefferson, and the awesome Columbia River Gorge. This route is very tough—make sure to bring plenty of food and water with you and watch out for scattered technical rocky sections (especially coming back down). Rest rooms and water are available at the trailhead. No water is available at the summit.

Finding the trailhead: From the intersection of I–205 and I–84 in Portland, drive 21

Mount Hood

miles east on I–84 to the Multnomah Falls exit (#31). Park in the large paved parking area at Multnomah Falls. To reach the trailhead, go through the tunnel and follow the broad paved steps, which lead you to the trailhead behind Multnomah Falls Lodge. *DeLorme: Oregon Atlas & Gazetteer:* Page 67 D8.

TRAIL DIRT

0.0 Start running on the paved path next to Multnomah Falls Lodge. As the trail climbs you'll contend with a series of stairs and crowds of people.

0.1 Pass a sign that states MULTNOMAH FALLS BRIDGE 0.2/TOP OF FALLS 1/WAHKEENAH TRAIL 1.8/LARCH MOUNTAIN 6.8.

0.2 Run (or walk depending how many people are here) across a magnificent bridge that spans Multnomah Creek and has a striking view of Multnomah Falls.

1.0 After reaching the top of the falls, the paved trail begins to descend a short distance until you arrive at a T intersection. Continue left on the dirt path. (The path that heads right leads to an overlook of the falls.) Cross a stone bridge over the creek. (After you cross the creek, the trail starts climbing up the scenic Multnomah Creek Canyon.)

1.1 Turn left onto Larch Mountain Trail #441.

1.7 Turn left on Larch Mountain Trail #441 at the sign LARCH MOUNTAIN 5. (Wahkeenah Trail #420 heads right at this junction.)

3.0 The singletrack trail intersects with a doubletrack road. Continue a short distance on the doubletrack to another trail junction. Turn right onto a singletrack trail at the sign LARCH MOUNTAIN TRAIL 4 MILES.

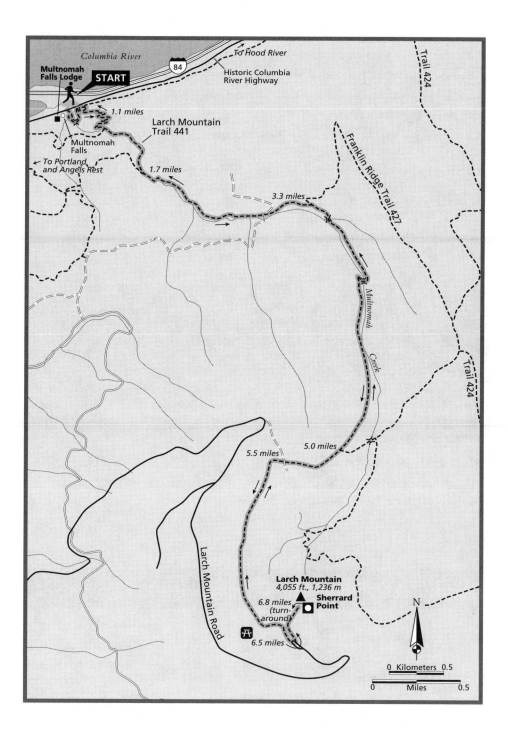

Columbia River

To Hood River

84

**Multnomah
Falls Lodge** START

Historic Columbia
River Highway

1.1 miles

Larch Mountain
Trail 441

Multnomah
Falls

To Portland
and Angels Rest

1.7 miles

3.3 miles

Franklin Ridge Trail 427

Trail 424

Multnomah Creek

5.0 miles

5.5 miles

Trail 424

Larch Mountain Road

Larch Mountain
4,055 ft., 1,236 m

**Sherrard
Point**

6.8 miles
(turn-
around)

6.5 miles

N

0 Kilometers 0.5

0 Miles 0.5

3.3 Continue straight (right). (Franklin Ridge Trail #427 goes left.)

5.0 Turn right at the trail fork.

5.5 Cross a doubletrack road and continue powering uphill.

6.5 Turn left at the trail fork.

6.6 Arrive at a paved parking area. Cross the parking area and pick up the paved trail toward Sherrard Point.

6.8 Arrive at the 4,055-foot summit of Larch Mountain at Sherrard Point. (From this spectacular summit you'll have views [on a clear day] of Mount Rainier, Mount St. Helens, Mount Adams, Mount Hood, Mount Jefferson, and the Columbia River Gorge.) From here, reverse the trail directions and begin a raging technical downhill back to your starting point.

13.6 Arrive at the trailhead.

Multnomah Falls is 642 feet high and is the fourth-highest year-round falls in the United States.

TRAIL FOOD

Black Rabbit Restaurant at McMenamins Edgefield, 2126 Southwest Halsey Street, Troutdale, OR 97060, (503) 492–3086, www.mcmenamins.com

Multnomah Falls Lodge Restaurant, 50000 Historic Columbia River Highway, Bridal Veil, OR 97010, (503) 695–2376, www.multnomahfallslodge.com

21: Horsetail-Ponytail-Oneonta-Triple Falls

Region/area:	Columbia River Gorge
Pain:	4
Gain:	4
Distance:	6.4 miles out and back
Elevation gain:	1,140 feet
Time:	1.25 to 2 hours

The route:	This route takes you past four scenic waterfalls and through a fabulous Oneonta Creek canyon in the Columbia River Gorge. Bridge crossings.
Trail surface:	45% smooth dirt, 55% rocky
Sun exposure:	5%
Runability:	95%
Season:	Year-round (the trail can be muddy and icy during the winter months)
Other users:	Hikers
Canine compatibility:	Leashed dogs permitted
Permits/fees:	None
Trail contact:	USDA Forest Service, Columbia River Gorge National Scenic Area, Hood River, OR, (541) 386–2333, www.fs.fed.us/r6/columbia
Maps:	USGS Multnomah Falls (7.5' series); USFS Trails of the Columbia River Gorge; Green Trails Bridal Veil

Trail scoop: This route takes you past four of the most beautiful waterfalls in the Columbia River Gorge. The route begins climbing steeply and you'll immediately be able to see the swishing action of 176-foot Horsetail Falls. After a short jaunt of steep climbing, you'll arrive at the refreshing cascade of Ponytail Falls, which plunges over a basalt ledge into a deep rock pool. The trail takes you behind the falls, so you can view the falls from a different perspective. As you continue cranking up the hill, you'll cross Oneonta Creek on a footbridge over stunning Oneonta Gorge and have a fantastic view of Oneonta Falls. After crossing the bridge the steep grade continues along Oneonta Creek past stunning canyon scenery. After 2.2 miles you'll arrive at a bridge that crosses Triple Falls. After crossing the bridge you'll continue on the trail as it heads uphill through an astounding mossy green forest for another mile to a footbridge crossing over Oneonta

Horsetail Falls

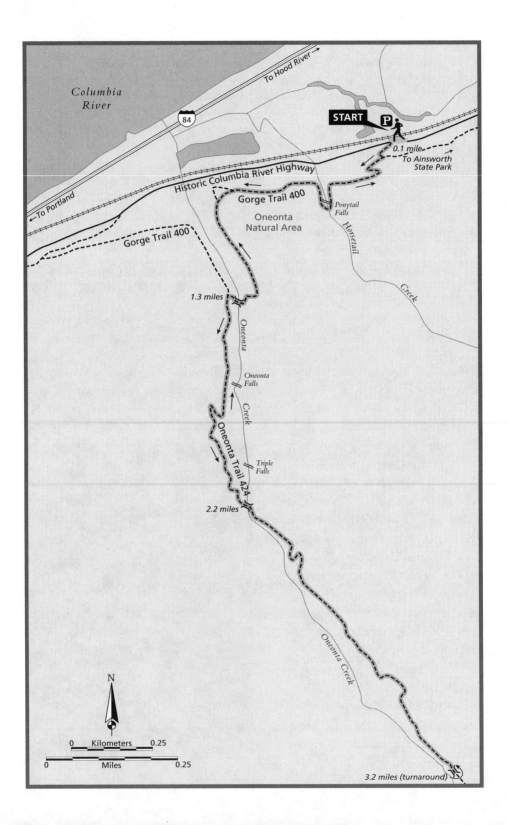

Columbia
River

To Hood River

84

START

P

0.1 mile
To Ainsworth
State Park

Historic Columbia River Highway

Gorge Trail 400

To Portland

Gorge Trail 400

Oneonta
Natural Area

Ponytail
Falls

Horsetail

Creek

1.3 miles

Oneonta

Oneonta
Falls

Creek

Oneonta Trail 424

Triple
Falls

2.2 miles

Oneonta Creek

N

0   Kilometers   0.25

0   Miles   0.25

3.2 miles (turnaround)

Creek (your turnaround point). No water or rest rooms are available at the trailhead.

Finding the trailhead: From Portland head approximately 33 miles east on I–84 to the Ainsworth exit (#35). Travel 1.5 miles west on the Historic Columbia River Highway and turn right into the Horsetail Falls parking area. *DeLorme: Oregon Atlas & Gazetteer:* Page 67 D8.

TRAIL DIRT

0.0 Start this route by crossing the Historic Columbia River Highway and powering uphill where a sign indicates UPPER HORSETAIL FALLS 0.4/VIEWPOINT 0.8/ONEONTA CREEK 1.2/ONEONTA TRAIL 1.3. (You'll immediately have a grand view of the long, swerving cascade of 176-foot Horsetail Falls.)

0.1 Turn right on Gorge Trail #400 where a sign reads PONYTAIL FALLS 0.2/ ONEONTA TRAIL 0.8. Continue uphill on a series of steep switchbacks as the trail passes through a shady big-leaf maple forest and fern-covered hillside.

0.4 Arrive at Ponytail Falls. This shimmering cascade drops over a basalt ledge into a deep rock pool. The trail leads you behind the falls through a cool basalt cave.

1.2 Cross over a metal bridge where you can glance at the brilliant 60-foot Oneonta Falls on your left. (Get ready to climb again on some steep switchbacks after you cross the bridge.)

1.3 Turn left at the ONEONTA TRAIL #424/HORSETAIL CREEK TRAIL 2.1 sign. (Gorge Trail #400 goes right at this junction.) Continue running on Oneonta Trail #424 as it winds steeply up gorgeous Oneonta Creek Canyon.

2.2 Arrive at a log bridge above Triple Falls and scenic Oneonta Creek. Cross the bridge and continue running on the trail as it continues uphill along the creek.

3.2 Arrive at another log bridge crossing Oneonta Creek (your turnaround point). Romp back downhill on the same route back to your starting point. *(Watch your footing on the descent. The rocks on this trail can be very wet and slippery.)*

6.4 Arrive at the trailhead.

TRAIL FOOD

Black Rabbit Restaurant at McMenamins Edgefield, 2126 Southwest Halsey Street, Troutdale, OR 97060, (503) 492–3086, www.mcmenamins.com

Multnomah Falls Lodge Restaurant, 50000 Historic Columbia River Highway, Bridal Veil, OR 97010, (503) 695–2376, www.multnomahfallslodge.com

22: Eagle Creek

Region/area:	Columbia River Gorge
Pain:	3
Gain:	5
Distance:	6 miles out and back (with longer options)
Elevation gain:	485 feet
Time:	1 to 1.5 hours
The route:	This trail travels through scenic Eagle Creek Canyon, carved by picturesque Eagle Creek in the Columbia River Gorge. Canyon views. Bridge crossings.
Trail surface:	95% smooth dirt, 5% rocky
Sun exposure:	75%
Runability:	100%
Season:	Year-round (the trail can be muddy and icy during the winter months)
Other users:	Hikers
Canine compatibility:	Leashed dogs permitted
Permits/fees:	$5.00 Northwest Forest Pass, purchased by calling (800) 270–7504, or online at www.naturenw.org. You can obtain a self-issue permit at the trailhead.
Trail contact:	USDA Forest Service, Columbia River Gorge National Scenic Area, Hood River, OR, (541) 386–2333, www.fs.fed.us/r6/columbia
Map:	USGS Bonneville Dam and Tanner Butte (7.5' series)

Trail scoop: This beautiful trail heads up Eagle Creek Canyon and is filled with spectacular scenery and waterfalls. You'll begin running at almost creek level but soon the trail begins climbing high above the creek and promises gorgeous scenery around every bend. There are a few precipitous sections on the trail, so watch your footing. Be forewarned that crowds flock to this trail during the summer months. For more solitude try this trail in the fall, when you can enjoy fantastic end-of-season colors. Rest rooms and water are available at the trailhead.

Finding the trailhead: From Portland head east on I–84 for about 41 miles. Take exit 41, Eagle Creek Recreation Area. At the stop sign, turn right and stay to the right toward the picnic area and trailhead. Drive about 0.5 mile to a paved parking area at the road's end.

From Hood River head west on I–84 and take Bonneville exit 40. Get back on

Eagle Creek

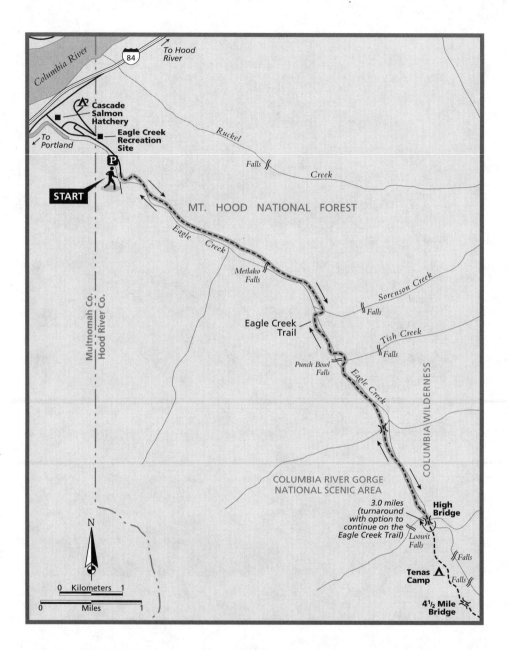

I–84 heading east. Take exit 41 for Eagle Creek Recreation Area. At the stop sign, turn right and stay to the right toward the picnic area and trailhead. Drive about 0.5 mile to a paved parking area at the road's end. *DeLorme: Oregon Atlas & Gazetteer:* Page 68 C1.

TRAIL DIRT

0.0 Start running on the signed singletrack trail that is lined with oak trees and parallels tumbling Eagle Creek.

0.8 The trail becomes precipitous and drops off steeply to the canyon floor. Watch your footing here! (As you head up this beautiful creek canyon there are options to head down side trails to view waterfalls, which abound in this canyon.)

3.0 Arrive at High Bridge—a steel bridge that gives you an amazing view of the narrow creek canyon far below you. This is your turnaround point. Retrace the route back to the trailhead. (**Option:** If you want to soak in more canyon scenery, this gorgeous trail continues another 10.3 miles to Wahtum Lake, which gives you a total round-trip journey of 26.6 miles.)

6.0 Arrive at the trailhead.

Waterfall Wonderland

The Columbia River Gorge has one of the highest concentrations of waterfalls in the United States. More than seventy-seven waterfalls make a roaring dive over basalt cliffs in a 420-square-mile area.

TRAIL FOOD

Full Sail Tasting Room & Pub, 506 Columbia Street, Hood River, OR 97031, (541) 386–2247, www.fullsailbrewing.com

Multnomah Falls Lodge Restaurant, 50000 Historic Columbia River Highway, Bridal Veil, OR 97010, (503) 695–2376, www.multnomahfallslodge.com

23: Deschutes River State Park Loop

Region/area:	Columbia River Gorge
Pain:	1
Gain:	3
Distance:	3.7-mile loop (with longer options)
Elevation gain:	75 feet
Time:	30 to 40 minutes
The route:	This loop route follows the shores of the swift-running Deschutes River in Deschutes River State Park and then

Deschutes River

	hooks up with the doubletrack rail-trail. River views. Creek crossings.
Trail surface:	93% smooth dirt, 5% rocky, and 2% sandy
Sun exposure:	95%
Runability:	99%
Season:	Year-round
Other users:	Hikers, mountain bikers, equestrians
Canine compatibility:	Leashed dogs permitted
Permits/fees:	$5.00 parking fee. Envelopes for the parking fee are available at the campground self-pay station.
Trail contact:	Oregon State Parks and Recreation, Salem, OR, (800) 551–6949, www.oregonstateparks.org/park_37.php
Maps:	USGS Emerson and Wishram (7.5' series); *Deschutes River State Park Trail* map, available from Oregon State Parks (800) 551–6949, www.oregonstateparks.org/park_37.php

Trail scoop: Go on a fun river romp as this trail rambles up the scenic Deschutes River Canyon. The trail mixes fast singletrack with a wide and smooth rail-trail that travels through a sage and rimrock canyon. Bring plenty of water and be prepared for scorching summer temperatures, which can reach 100 degrees. Rest rooms are available at the trailhead. Water is available in the campground.

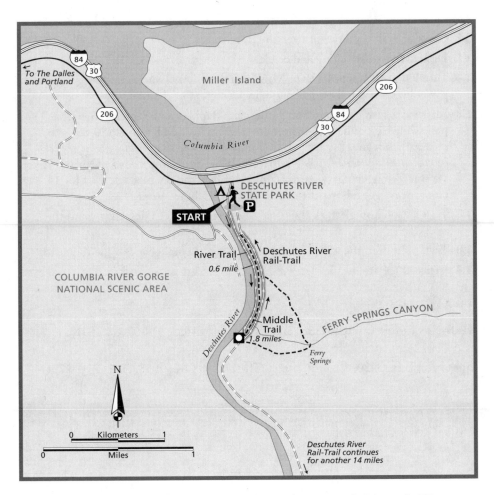

Finding the trailhead: From The Dalles travel 14 miles east on I–84 to exit 97, Highway 206/Celilo Park/Deschutes River State Park. Turn right at the end of the off-ramp and take an immediate left onto Highway 206. Head east for 3.1 miles and turn right into the entrance for Deschutes River State Park. Proceed 0.4 mile on the paved road through the campground to where it dead-ends at the trailhead sign. *DeLorme: Oregon Atlas & Gazetteer:* Page 84 B1.

TRAIL DIRT

0.0 Start running across a large grassy field paralleling the scenic Deschutes River.

0.1 Arrive at a wood trail sign that indicates the River Trail is to the right and the Middle and Upper Trails are to the left. Go right and begin running on the smooth singletrack of the River Trail.

0.6 Continue straight (right) on the River Trail. (The Middle Trail goes left at this intersection.)

0.7 Cross several wood ramps over a marshy area.

1.2 Dash over a small spring-fed creek.

1.4 Turn left at the UPPER TRAIL/MIDDLE TRAIL sign. Switch into low gear and power up a steep hill over a rough, rocky section of the trail.

1.8 Arrive at a scenic overlook of Rattlesnake Rapids and an interpretive sign. The trail swings left and then down a short, rocky section for about 50 yards to a doubletrack road. *(You may want to walk the last several yards down to the road because of the numerous rocks.)* Turn left on the doubletrack road. (**Option:** If you are still feeling energetic, turn right and follow the doubletrack road for 14 more miles as it follows the course of the Deschutes River.)

3.5 Turn left on a singletrack trail that takes you on a steep descent toward the river.

3.6 Turn right onto the wide grassy field and run 0.1 mile back to the trailhead.

3.7 Arrive at the trailhead.

TRAIL FOOD

Holsteins Coffee Company, 3rd and Taylor, The Dalles, OR 97058, (541) 298–2326

Spooky's Pizza, 3320 West 6th Street, The Dalles, OR 97058, (541) 298–2211

Hood River/Mount Hood

H ood River is the gateway to the Hood River Valley and the 1.2-million-acre Mount Hood National Forest. This amazing national forest has four designated wilderness areas and boasts more that 1,200 miles of fabulous trails to explore. The star attraction of the Mount Hood National Forest is 11,239-foot Mount Hood—Oregon's tallest peak. The first white men "discovered" the mountain on October 29, 1792, when British Naval Lt. William Broughton and his crew (representing King George III) saw it from the Columbia River. Broughton named the peak for famed British naval officer Alexander Arthur Hood. Recommended trails that promise wonderful views of snow-capped Mount Hood include Lost Lake, Mirror Lake, and Timothy Lake. For a pristine river run, check out the Salmon River Trail that traipses along the Salmon River through the Salmon-Huckleberry Wilderness.

Region/area:	Hood River/Mount Hood
Pain:	2
Gain:	3
Distance:	4 miles out and back
Elevation gain:	500 feet
Time:	35 minutes to 1 hour
The route:	This singletrack route crosses the East Fork of Hood River, parallels bouldery Cold Spring Creek, and takes you to the magnificent cascade of Tamanawas Falls. Bridge crossings.
Trail surface:	80% smooth dirt, 20% rocky
Sun exposure:	15%
Runability:	95%
Season:	April through November
Other users:	Hikers, mountain bikers (on East Fork of Hood River Trail only)
Canine compatibility:	Dogs permitted
Permits/fees:	$5.00 Northwest Forest Pass, purchased by calling (800) 270–7504, or online at www.naturenw.org.
Trail contact:	Mount Hood National Forest Headquarters Office, Sandy, OR, (503) 622–7674, www.fs.fed.us/r6/mthood
Maps:	USGS Dog River (7.5' series); USFS Mount Hood Wilderness; Green Trails Mount Hood

Finding the trailhead: From I–84 in Hood River, take exit 64. Turn south onto Highway 35 and travel 25.3 miles into a gravel parking area at the trailhead on the right side of the road.

From Portland head about 56 miles east on U.S. Highway 26 to the intersection with Highway 35. Turn north onto Highway 35 and travel about 15 miles to a gravel parking area and the trailhead on the left side of the road (0.2 mile north of Sherwood Campground). *DeLorme: Oregon Atlas & Gazetteer:* Page 62 A4.

Trail scoop: This trail takes you through the cool, watery world of the Hood River Basin, filled with towering Douglas fir trees, mossy creeks, and the splashing coolness of Tamanawas Falls. No rest rooms or water are available at the trailhead.

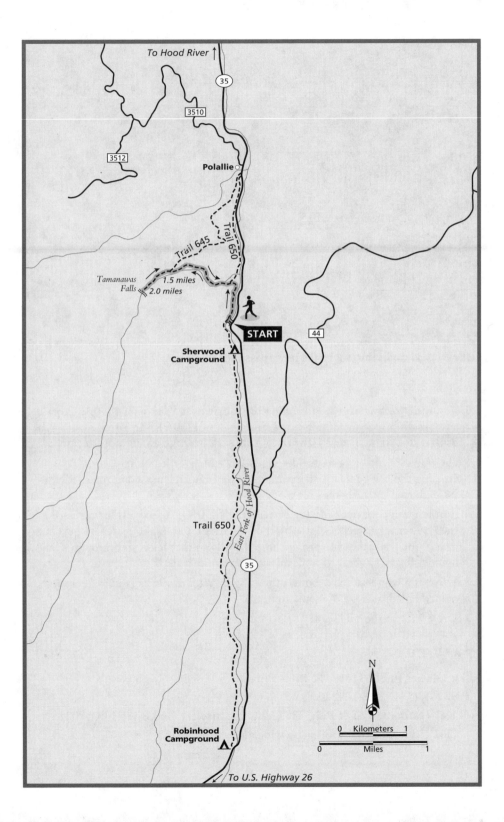

To Hood River ↑

35

3510

3512

Polallie

Trail 645

Trail 650

Tamanawas Falls

1.5 miles
2.0 miles

START

Sherwood Campground

44

Trail 650

East Fork of Hood River

35

Robinhood Campground

To U.S. Highway 26

N

Kilometers
0 — 1

Miles
0 — 1

Getting a good cardio workout on the Tamanawas Falls Trail

TRAIL DIRT

0.0 From the parking area start running on Tamanawas Falls Trail #650A. Cross a suspension bridge over the roaring East Fork of Hood River. After crossing the bridge turn right at the TAMANAWAS FALLS 2/POLLALIE CAMPGROUND sign.

0.5 The trail descends to a footbridge across splashing Cold Spring Creek. After crossing the bridge take a sharp left and continue cruising along the shady forest path as it parallels the creek.

1.5 Turn left and continue on Tamanawas Trail #650A. Proceed a short distance and then power up a steep rocky section of the trail for about 50 feet. The next section of the trail takes you around an old washout that takes you through a large boulder field. It is best to walk this section of the trail.

2.0 Arrive at a wonderful viewpoint of roaring Tamanawas Falls (your turnaround point). Head back on the same route.

4.0 Arrive back at the trailhead.

TRAIL FOOD

Elliot Glacier Public House & Brew Pub, 4945 Baseline Road, Parkdale, OR 97041, (541) 352–1022

Full Sail Tasting Room & Pub, 506 Columbia Street, Hood River, OR 97031, (541) 386–2247, www.fullsailbrewing.com

25: East Fork of Hood River

Region/area:	Hood River/Mount Hood
Pain:	3
Gain:	3
Distance:	10.8 miles out and back
Elevation gain:	500 feet
Time:	2 to 2.5 hours
The route:	This trail parallels the East Fork of Hood River in the Mount Hood National Forest. River views. Bridge crossings.
Trail surface:	95% smooth dirt, 5% sand
Sun exposure:	60%
Runability:	100%
Season:	Mid-June through October
Other users:	Hikers, mountain bikers
Canine compatibility:	Dogs permitted
Permits/fees:	$5.00 Northwest Forest Pass, purchased by calling (800) 270–7504, or online at www.naturenw.org.
Trail contact:	Mount Hood National Forest Headquarters Office, Sandy, OR, (503) 622–7674, www.fs.fed.us/r6/mthood
Map:	USGS Dog River and Badger Lake (7.5' series)

Trail scoop: Sail along the shores of the East Fork of Hood River on this fantastic river run. Cool forest canopy, rushing water, and a rambling trail are all you need for a day of brilliant dirt running. The only obstacles on this route are mountain bikers who may buzz you on the trail. Rest rooms and water are not available at the trailhead.

Finding the trailhead: From I–84 in Hood River, take exit 64. Turn south onto Highway 35 and travel 25.3 miles into a gravel parking area at the trailhead on the right side of the road.

From Portland head about 56 miles east on U.S. Highway 26 to the intersection with Highway 35. Turn north onto Highway 35 and travel about 15 miles to a gravel parking area and the trailhead on the left side of the road (0.2 mile north of Sherwood Campground.) *DeLorme: Oregon Atlas & Gazetteer:* Page 62 A4.

Crossing over the East Fork of Hood River

TRAIL DIRT

0.0 Start this fast singletrack route by crossing the narrow wood bridge over the East Fork of Hood River. After you cross the bridge, turn left (south) on the singletrack trail #650. (The trail sweeps along the ridge above the river. You'll have fun cranking up short hills that have many curly-fry turns and then blasting down the trail as it follows the contour of the ridge.)

3.9 *(At this point the trail is close to the river's edge and can be very sandy and soft in spots.)*

5.1 (You'll sail through a thick forest and cross many wood ramps over marshy areas for the next 0.3 mile.)

5.4 Arrive at Robinhood Campground and your turnaround point. From here, reverse the trail directions back to the trailhead.

10.8 Arrive at the trailhead.

TRAIL FOOD

Elliot Glacier Public House & Brew Pub, 4945 Baseline Road, Parkdale, OR 97041, (541) 352–1022

Full Sail Tasting Room & Pub, 506 Columbia Street, Hood River, OR 97031, (541) 386–2247, www.fullsailbrewing.com

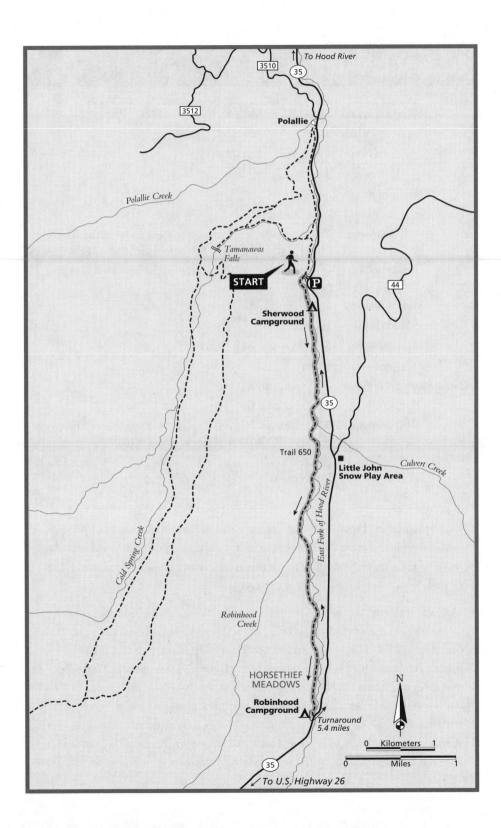

To Hood River

3510
35

3512

Polallie

Polallie Creek

Tamanawas Falls

START

P

Sherwood Campground

44

35

Trail 650

Little John Snow Play Area

Culvert Creek

East Fork of Hood River

Cold Spring Creek

Robinhood Creek

HORSETHIEF MEADOWS

Robinhood Campground

Turnaround 5.4 miles

N

0   Kilometers   1

0   Miles   1

35

To U.S. Highway 26

26: Lost Lake Loop

Region/area:	Hood River/Mount Hood
Pain:	1
Gain:	4
Distance:	3-mile loop
Elevation gain:	None
Time:	20 to 30 minutes
The route:	This route circles picturesque Lost Lake in the Mount Hood National Forest. Mountain views. Bridge crossings.
Trail surface:	75% smooth dirt, 10% paved path, 5% rocky, 10% wood ramps
Sun exposure:	5%
Runability:	100%
Season:	Mid-May through October
Other users:	Hikers
Canine compatibility:	Dogs permitted
Permits/fees:	$5.00 parking fee
Trail contact:	Mount Hood National Forest Headquarters Office, Sandy, OR, (503) 622–7674, www.fs.fed.us/r6/mthood
Maps:	USGS Bull Run Lake (7.5' series); USFS Mount Hood Wilderness

Trail scoop: Enjoy smooth sailing around picturesque Lost Lake on this classic lake route in the Mount Hood National Forest. Perks include stellar views of Mount Hood, old-growth forest, and opportunities for swimming on a hot summer's day. Beware of the slippery wood ramps on this route. Rest rooms are available at the trailhead. Water is available in the campground.

Finding the trailhead: From the intersection of I–205 and I–84 in Portland head east for 7.2 miles on I–84 to exit 13, 238th Drive/Wood Village. Turn right onto 238th Drive, proceed 2.9 miles, and turn left onto Burnside Road. Travel 1 mile on Burnside Road and turn left (east) onto U.S. Highway 26. Continue 27.5 miles east to the town of Zigzag. At the Zigzag Store turn left (north) onto East Lolo Pass Road. Travel 10.9 miles to the intersection with the unsigned gravel Forest Service Road 1810 (McKee Creek Road). (This road is the first right turn after the signed Forest Service Road 828.) Turn right onto Forest Service Road 1810 (McKee Creek Road) and continue for 7.5 miles until the road intersects with Forest Service Road 18. Continue on paved Forest Road 18 for 7 miles on pavement to the intersection with Forest Service Road 13. Turn left on Forest Service Road 13 and travel 6 miles to the pay booth at Lost Lake. After the entry booth stay to the right as the road parallels the lake. Continue past the general store to the road's end at a day-use picnic area.

From I–84 in Hood River, take exit 62, West Hood River. Travel about a mile into Hood River and take a right onto 13th Street. Travel approximately 3.5 miles to Odell. Cross a bridge and turn right after Tucker Park and travel 6.3 miles. Stay to the right toward Dee. From the small town of Dee, travel 14 miles, following signs to Lost Lake. After the pay booth at the lake, stay to the right as

Sage setting the pace at Lost Lake

the road parallels the lake. Continue past the general store to the road's end at a day-use picnic area. *DeLorme: Oregon Atlas & Gazetteer:* Page 62 A2.

TRAIL DIRT

0.0 From the parking area begin running in a counterclockwise direction around the lake on Lakeshore Trail #656. (Make a note of the intersection where the parking lot access trail meets the Lakeshore Trail. This will be your exit trail after you finish the lake loop. The path is wide, smooth, and fast, and it travels through a shady forest canopy of cedar and hemlock trees. If you look across the lake through the shady canopy of trees, you'll have a picturesque view of Mount Hood.)

0.6 Cross a boardwalk that travels through a marshy area filled with skunk cabbage and other marsh grasses.

1.8 Arrive at a trail intersection with the signed Huckleberry Mountain Trail. Stay to the left and continue on the Lakeshore Trail. Run another 100 yards to another trail junction with the sign To OLD-GROWTH TRAIL/GROUP CAMP/ DAY-USE AREA 1 MILE. Veer left.

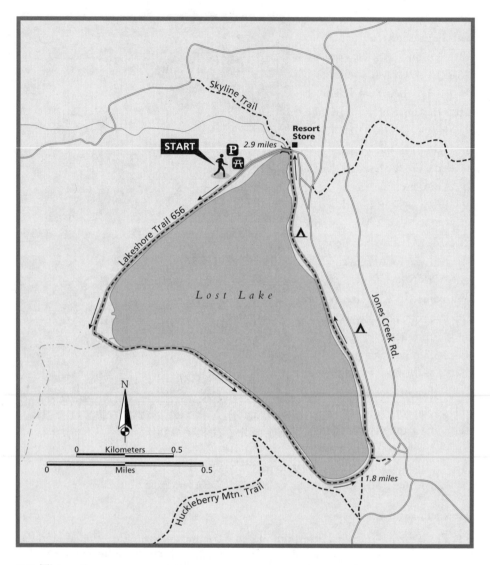

2.5 The trail turns to pavement.

2.8 The paved path intersects with a paved road at an unsigned junction. Veer left and continue running on a gravel path.

2.9 Cross a footbridge over Lake Branch Creek.

3.0 Turn right and power up a short set of stairs and arrive back at the parking area and your starting point.

TRAIL FOOD

Elusive Trout Pub, 39333 Proctor Boulevard, Sandy, OR 97055, (503) 668–7884

Region/area:	Hood River/Mount Hood
Pain:	2
Gain:	4
Distance:	11.4-mile loop
Elevation gain:	None
Time:	2.25 to 3 hours
The route:	A zippy singletrack trail that follows the shores of Timothy Lake in the Mount Hood National Forest. Mountain views. Bridge crossings.
Trail surface:	85% smooth dirt, 2% paved, 13% rocky
Sun exposure:	25%
Runability:	100%
Season:	Mid-June through October
Other users:	Hikers, mountain bikers, equestrians
Canine compatibility:	Leashed dogs permitted
Permits/fees:	None
Trail contact:	Mount Hood National Forest Headquarters Office, Sandy, OR, (503) 622–7674, www.fs.fed.us/r6/mthood
Maps:	USGS Timothy Lake and Wolf Peak (7.5' series); Green Trails High Rock

Trail scoop: It's hard to beat running on smooth singletrack around a pristine high-alpine lake. This trail soars around the shores of Timothy Lake through a cool forest. Plenty of opportunities are available to dive into the lake on a hot summer's day. No water or rest rooms are available at the trailhead.

Finding the trailhead: From the intersection of I–205 and I–84 in Portland, head east for 7.2 miles on I–84 to exit 13, 238th Drive/Wood Village. At the end of the off-ramp, turn right on 238th Avenue and proceed 2.9 miles to the intersection with Burnside Road. Turn left onto Burnside Road and proceed to the intersection with U.S. Highway 26. Turn left (east) onto U.S Highway 26 and go 51.4 miles to the junction with Forest Service Road 42 (Skyline Road). Turn right on Forest Service Road 42 and travel 8.3 miles to the junction with Forest Service Road 57. Turn right onto Forest Service Road 57 and go 3.6 miles (passing four campgrounds on your right) and cross over the dam. After you cross the dam turn right and travel 0.1 mile to a road intersection. Turn right on a gravel road and drive 0.1 mile to the Timothy Lake Trail #528 trailhead parking area. *DeLorme: Oregon Atlas & Gazetteer:* Page 62 D2.

An extra perk on the Timothy Lake Trail

TRAIL DIRT

0.0 Start running in a clockwise direction on Timothy Lake Trail #528 at the MEDIATION POINT 1.5 MILES/PACIFIC CREST TRAIL 4.5 MILES sign.

1.1 Continue cruising straight on Timothy Lake Trail #528. (Trail #526 for Meditation Point Campground goes right at this junction.)

3.3 Arrive at a junction with a gravel road. Turn left and go about 100 yards. Turn right and keep cruising on the signed Timothy Lake Trail #528.

4.2 Turn right and continue on Timothy Lake Trail #528. A sign states BICYCLISTS DISMOUNT FOR 600 FEET TO OLD 1916 TRAIL #537.

4.5 Continue straight on the Pacific Crest Trail #2000 and follow it south.

8.3 Turn right and continue on the smooth and fast Timothy Lake Trail #528.

9.6 Continue straight on Timothy Lake Trail #528. (Over the next 1.5 miles, you'll

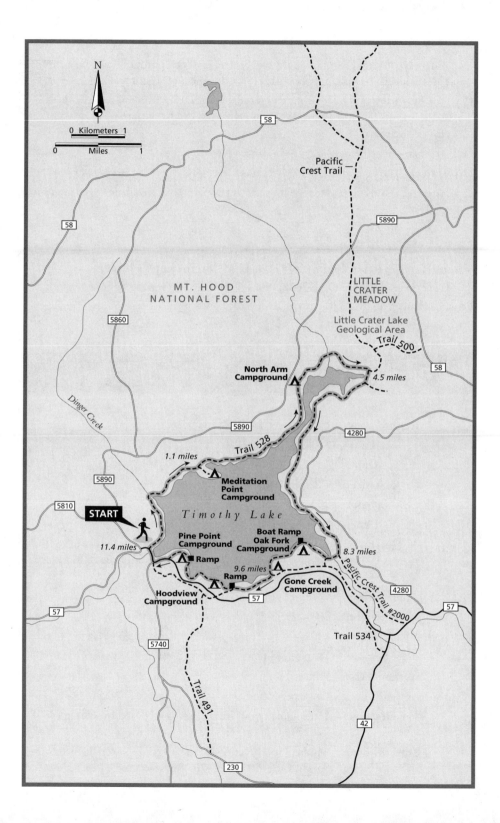

N

0 Kilometers 1
0 Miles 1

58

Pacific
Crest Trail

58

5890

MT. HOOD
NATIONAL FOREST

LITTLE
CRATER
MEADOW

5860

Little Crater Lake
Geological Area

Trail 500

58

North Arm
Campground

4.5 miles

Dinger Creek

5890

Trail 528

4280

1.1 miles

5890

Meditation
Point
Campground

5810

START

Timothy Lake

Boat Ramp
Oak Fork
Campground

8.3 miles

11.4 miles

Pine Point
Campground

Ramp

9.6 miles
Ramp

Pacific Crest Trail #2000

4280

57

Hoodview
Campground

57

Gone Creek
Campground

57

5740

Trail 534

Trail 491

42

230

glide next to the lakeshore and travel past several campgrounds and boat ramps. You'll also have many opportunities to view majestic Mount Hood.)

11.1 Pass by a fishing dock on your right and then the trail turns to pavement. Run about 100 yards on the paved trail and then turn right onto the paved road that crosses the dam.

11.2 After crossing the dam turn right onto a paved road.

11.3 Turn right onto an unsigned gravel road.

11.4 Arrive at the trailhead. Celebrate your finish by taking a well-deserved swim in the lake!

TRAIL FOOD

Mount Hood Brewing Company, 87304 East Government Camp Loop, Government Camp, OR 97028, (503) 622–0724, www.mthoodbrewing.com

Elusive Trout Pub, 39333 Proctor Boulevard, Sandy, OR 97055, (503) 668–7884

28: Salmon River

Region/area:	Hood River/Mount Hood
Pain:	3
Gain:	4
Distance:	7.2-mile loop
Elevation gain:	900 feet
Time:	1.5 to 2 hours
The route:	A fantastic river route that hugs the contours of the Salmon River and then climbs to a high ridge to a scenic viewpoint. Views. Bridges.
Trail surface:	90% smooth dirt, 10% rocky
Sun exposure:	20%
Runability:	100%
Season:	Year-round (snow can be present in the winter months)
Other users:	Hikers
Canine compatibility:	Dogs permitted
Permits/fees:	$5.00 Northwest Forest Pass, purchased by calling (800) 270–7504, or online at www.naturenw.org.
Trail contact:	Mount Hood National Forest Headquarters Office, Sandy, OR, (503) 622–7674, www.fs.fed.us/r6/mthood
Map:	USGS Rhododendron (7.5' series)

A runner's paradise on the Salmon River Trail

Trail scoop: This beautiful river trail takes you on a tranquil journey through the Salmon River Canyon past old-growth red cedars and Douglas fir. After 2 miles the trail turns away from the river and switchbacks up a high ridge with great views of the canyon. You'll complete a short loop and then return on the same trail. No water or rest rooms are available at the trailhead.

Finding the trailhead: From Portland travel 42 miles east on U.S. Highway 26 to Zigzag. Turn right (south) onto Salmon River Road and travel 4.9 miles to the parking area and trailhead on the left side of the road. *DeLorme: Oregon Atlas & Gazetteer:* Page 62 B1.

TRAIL DIRT

0.0 Start on the singletrack trail located on the far end of the parking area next to the bridge. The trail takes you close to the river through big old-growth cedars and Douglas fir trees.

2.0 Cross a footbridge and arrive at a self-issue wilderness permit station. Take a breather and fill out a wilderness permit and then continue your journey.

3.4 Turn right to begin a short loop.

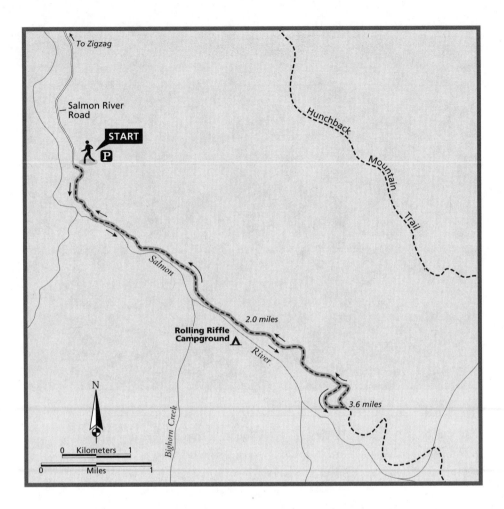

3.5 You'll exit out of the trees onto a grassy ridge with spectacular views of the river canyon. *(Watch your footing on the trail—it can be loose and slippery.)*

3.6 Turn left at a T junction.

3.8 The loop section of the trail ends. Veer right and retrace the route back to the trailhead.

7.2 Arrive at the trailhead.

TRAIL FOOD

Elusive Trout Pub, 39333 Proctor Boulevard, Sandy, OR 97055, (503) 668–7884

29: Mirror Lake Loop

Region/area:	Hood River/Mount Hood
Pain:	2
Gain:	4
Distance:	3.2-mile loop
Elevation gain:	700 feet
Time:	40 minutes to 1 hour
The route:	A singletrack trail that travels through a pine-scented forest to a scenic alpine lake with gorgeous views of Mount Hood.
Trail surface:	95% smooth dirt, 5% rocky
Sun exposure:	25%
Runability:	100%
Season:	Mid-May through mid-November
Other users:	Hikers
Canine compatibility:	Dogs permitted
Permits/fees:	$5.00 Northwest Forest Pass, purchased by calling (800) 270–7504, or online at www.naturenw.org.
Trail contact:	Mount Hood National Forest Headquarters Office, Sandy, OR, (503) 622–7674, www.fs.fed.us/r6/mthood
Maps:	USGS Government Camp (7.5' series); USFS Mount Hood Wilderness

Trail scoop: This trail has everything you ever wanted: a good cardio pump, a smooth trail, a bubbling creek and scenic alpine lake, a killer view of Mount Hood, wild-flowers, and cool, shady forest. If it sounds too good to be true, there is a catch—it is very popular and very crowded (especially on summer weekends). If you can look past the crowds, you'll love the run to this high-alpine lake that offers prime swimming opportunities in mid-summer.

Finding the trailhead: From the intersection of I–205 and I–84 in Portland head east for 7.2 miles on I–84 to exit 13, 238th Drive/Wood Village. Turn right onto 238th Drive and proceed 2.9 miles. Turn left onto Burnside Road. Continue about a mile and turn left (east) onto U.S. Highway 26. Travel east on U.S Highway 26 to an unmarked trailhead between mileposts 51 and 52 on the right (south) side of the highway.

From Hood River head south on Highway 35 to the junction with U.S. Highway 26. Turn right (west) onto U.S. Highway 26 and travel west to

Along Mirror Lake with Mount Hood in the background

Government Camp. From Government Camp continue approximately 2 miles west on U.S. Highway 26 to an unmarked trailhead on the left (south) side of the highway between mileposts 51 and 52. *DeLorme: Oregon Atlas & Gazetteer:* Page 62 B2.

TRAIL DIRT

0.0 Head across a footbridge across bubbling Camp Creek and hook up with the smooth and wide Mirror Lake Trail. Power uphill on a series of switchbacks through a cool, shady forest.

1.4 Arrive at a T intersection and the beginning of the signed Mirror Lake Loop Trail. Turn right and circle the lake in a counterclockwise direction. At the next trail junction, stay to the left and continue on the loop around the lake, which is dotted with deep purple lupine, vibrant Indian paintbrush, and other colorful wildflowers. (You may have to dodge people and dogs on this popular lake loop. As you cruise around the lake look across the lake to catch some awesome views of Mount Hood.)

1.8 You'll end the loop portion of the route. Turn right and zip downhill on the same route back to your starting point.

3.2 Arrive at the trailhead.

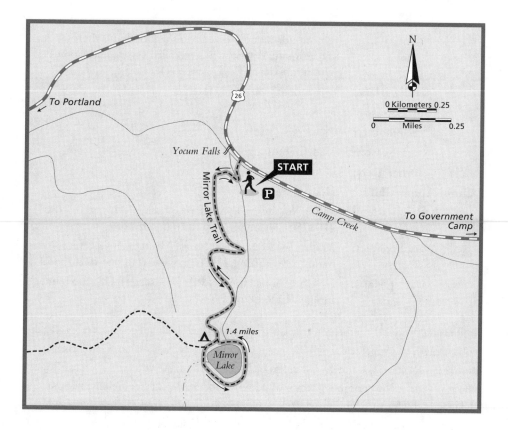

TRAIL FOOD

Mount Hood Brewing Company, 87304 East Government Camp Loop,
Government Camp, OR 97028, (503) 622–0724, www.mthoodbrewing.com
Elusive Trout Pub, 39333 Proctor Boulevard, Sandy, OR 97055, (503) 668–7884

30: Vista Ridge–Cairn Basin–Eden Park Loop

Region/area:	Hood River/Mount Hood
Pain:	4
Gain:	3
Distance:	8.3-mile loop
Elevation gain:	1,700 feet
Time:	2 to 2.5 hours
The route:	This challenging loop trail climbs Vista Ridge on the

remote northwest side of Mount Hood and then takes you through Wy'East Basin, Cairn Basin, and Eden Park. Mountain views. Bridgeless creek crossings.

Trail surface:	85% smooth dirt, 15% rocky
Sun exposure:	35%
Runability:	99%
Season:	Mid-July through October
Other users:	Hikers
Canine compatibility:	Dogs permitted
Permits/fees:	$5.00 Northwest Forest Pass, purchased by calling (800) 270–7504, or online at www.naturenw.org.
Trail contact:	Mount Hood National Forest Headquarters Office, Sandy, OR, (503) 622–7674, www.fs.fed.us/r6/mthood
Maps:	USGS Mount Hood North (7.5' series); USFS Mount Hood Wilderness

Trail scoop: Way off the beaten track, this adventurous and challenging trail will take you through the spectacular wildflower meadows of Wy'East Basin, Cairn Basin, and Eden Park on the northwest ridge of Mount Hood. As you climb Vista Ridge, you'll have brief but gorgeous views of Mount Hood, Mount St. Helens, Mount Adams, and Mount Rainier. Additional challenges on this trail include two bridgeless crossings over rumbling Ladd Creek. This creek may be too treacherous to cross during high runoff periods.

Finding the trailhead: From the intersection of I–205 and I–84 in Portland, head east 7.2 miles on I–84 to exit 13, 238th Drive/Wood Village. Turn right onto 238th Drive and proceed 2.9 miles. Turn left onto Burnside Road. After 1 mile this turns into U.S. Highway 26. Continue 27.5 miles east on U.S. Highway 26 to the town of Zigzag. Just after the Zigzag Store, turn left (north) onto East Lolo Pass Road. Travel 10.9 miles to an intersection with the unsigned gravel Forest Service Road 1810 (McKee Creek Road). (This road is right after the signed Forest Service 828 Road.) Turn right onto Forest Service Road 1810 (McKee Creek Road) and proceed 7.5 miles until the road intersects with Forest Service Road 18. Continue on paved Forest Service Road 18 for 3.3 miles to the junction with Forest Service Road 16. Turn right onto Forest Service Road 16 at the VISTA RIDGE TRAIL #626—8 MILES sign. Follow paved Forest Service Road 16 for 5.7 miles to a road junction with Forest Service Road 1650. Take a very sharp right onto Forest Service Road 1650 (the road turns to gravel here) and drive 2.8 miles to a road intersection. Stay to the left and continue to follow the signs for the Vista Ridge Trail for another 0.9 mile to the trailhead. *DeLorme: Oregon Atlas & Gazetteer:* Page 62 A3.

Balancing act over Ladd Creek

TRAIL DIRT

0.0 Start running uphill on Vista Ridge Trail #626 through a shady hemlock and Douglas fir forest. (*You need to fill out a self-issue wilderness permit at the start of the run. You'll have to negotiate some rock gardens the first 0.2 mile.*)

0.4 Turn right and continue running on Vista Ridge Trail #626. A sign indicates you'll reach Timberline Trail in 2.5 miles. (At this point you'll be running up the moderately steep spine of Vista Ridge.)

2.7 Turn left on the Vista Ridge Trail #626 where a sign indicates Elk Cove. (At this point you'll have spectacular views of Mount Adams, Mount Saint Helens, Mount Hood, and Mount Rainier. You'll also pass through a profusion of wildflowers that begin blooming in early August.)

3.0 You'll run through the green meadowy bowl of Wy'East Basin to another trail junction. Turn right toward Cairn Basin. Continue powering up the ridge while admiring the awesome mountain views. Eventually you'll have to negotiate some steep and tricky switchbacks down to a bridgeless crossing at rumbling Ladd Creek. This crossing changes every year during the spring thaw. Take care hopping across the boulders and logs. Head upstream a short ways for the continuation of the trail.

4.1 Arrive in Cairn Basin and a stone shelter on your left. Veer right and continue running on the main trail, which is lined with large stones. At the next trail junction (beside a small creek) turn right toward Eden Park.

4.5 Arrive at the open meadows of Eden Park. (*Watch your footing on this section of the trail—it is very uneven and rocky.*) After admiring Eden Park get ready to

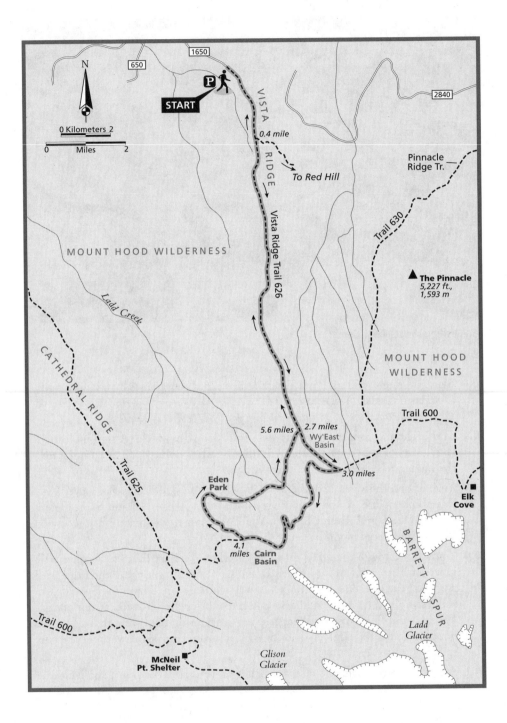

N

650

1650

P

START

VISTA RIDGE

0.4 mile

To Red Hill

2840

Pinnacle Ridge Tr.

Trail 630

0 Kilometers 2

0 Miles 2

MOUNT HOOD WILDERNESS

Ladd Creek

Vista Ridge Trail 626

The Pinnacle
5,227 ft.,
1,593 m

CATHEDRAL RIDGE

MOUNT HOOD WILDERNESS

Trail 600

Trail 625

5.6 miles

2.7 miles
Wy'East Basin

3.0 miles

Eden Park

Elk Cove

4.1 miles

Cairn Basin

BARRETT SPUR

Trail 600

McNeil Pt. Shelter

Glison Glacier

Ladd Glacier

gear down for another bridgeless crossing of the raging Ladd Creek. (Picking up the trail on the other side can be a little tricky. Look for the trail as it heads uphill paralleling the creek.)

5.6 Turn left on Vista Ridge Trail and enjoy a fun spin down Vista Ridge.

7.9 Turn left and continue on the Vista Ridge Trail.

8.3 Arrive at the trailhead.

TRAIL FOOD

Mount Hood Brewing Company, 87304 East Government Camp Loop, Government Camp, OR 97028, (503) 622–0724, www.mthoodbrewing.com

Elusive Trout Pub, 39333 Proctor Boulevard, Sandy, OR 97055, (503) 668–7884

Willamette Valley

On the western side of the Cascade Mountains, the Willamette Valley dominates the northern part of the state with its miles of fertile farmland, wide river valleys, and rolling foothills. Many of Oregon's largest cities are located in the Willamette Valley, and they are surrounded by city, county, and state parks that offer a variety of trails that are easy to get to and offer a variety of challenges. Salem's Minto–Brown Island Park has twenty-plus miles of trails to explore in a pastoral setting adjacent to the Willamette River, and Silver Falls State Park promises an exhilarating trail run past gorgeous waterfalls. Eugene's Ridgeline Trail System takes you through grand old Douglas firs and challenges you with its undulating track. Those looking for a good hill workout will also enjoy running to the summit of Mount Pisgah, located just outside Eugene's city limits. Dan's Trail, located in the McDonald Dunn Research Forest outside of Corvallis, takes you through a scenic forest to the top of 1,495-foot Dimple Hill. The Larison Creek and Salmon Creek Trails outside of Oakridge offer awesome scenery and a good workout. Another trail-running adventure that should not be missed is the magical McKenzie River Trail, which sweeps its way along the crystal-clear waters of the McKenzie River for more than 29 miles.

Region/area:	Salem
Pain:	1
Gain:	2
Distance:	5.8-mile loop (with other options)
Elevation gain:	5 feet
Time:	1 hour
The route:	This route treads on paved bike paths and wood-chip trails through Minto–Brown Island Park in Salem. Willamette River views.
Trail surface:	40% wood chip, 5% dirt, 55% paved
Sun exposure:	65%
Runability:	100%
Season:	Year-round (certain parts of the route may be muddy or flooded during the winter months)
Other users:	Hikers, cyclists
Canine compatibility:	Leashed dogs permitted
Permits/fees:	None
Trail contact:	Salem Parks Administration Recreation Office, 3rd floor, City Hall, Salem, OR, (503) 588–6261, www.open.org/~parks/minto_brown.htm
Map:	USGS Salem West (7.5' series)

Trail scoop: This loop route features views of the Willamette River, cool shady forest, open sunny pastures, and opportunities to view amazing bird life. A signboard at the trailhead lists designated running routes with route maps. If you still have some steam left after running this route, you may want to take another spin on one of the other loop trails. Rest rooms are available at the trailhead. No water is available.

Finding the trailhead: From I–5 in south Salem, take exit 252, Kuebler Boulevard. Turn west onto Kuebler Avenue and travel 2 miles. Turn right (north) onto Commercial Street. Continue north for 3.5 miles (after 3 miles Commercial Street turns into Liberty Street). Turn left onto Bush Street. Go 1 block and turn left onto Commercial Street, heading south. Proceed to the next light and turn right onto Owens Street. Go 1.2 miles on Owens Street (which turns into River Road) and turn right onto Minto Island Road. Go 0.2 mile and turn right into a paved parking area and the trailhead. *DeLorme: Oregon Atlas & Gazetteer:* Page 53 A8.

TRAIL DIRT

0.0 Begin running on the paved trail that starts to the left of the rest rooms at the far end of the parking area.

0.1 Cross over a wood bridge and arrive at an intersection with a paved road. Turn right and continue running on the paved route marked by a BIKE ROUTE sign.

0.3 Turn left at the trail junction and continue cruising on the paved trail.

0.6 Turn right at the trail junction and continue sailing on the flat paved path and enter a shady corridor of stately cottonwood trees. (This is a yummy blackberry area—they ripen starting in mid-August.)

1.3 Turn right at the trail junction and continue on the paved path that passes through a large grove of cottonwoods.

Our canine friends make great running partners.

1.5 The paved path parallels the Willamette River. If you don't want to run on the paved path, there is a softer dirt path that parallels the paved trail. (Watch for dusky Canada geese, blue herons, and other birds along this section of the route.)

2.1 Continue to the left (away from the river) on the paved trail (a dirt trail heads right).

2.2 Arrive at a T intersection with a paved trail. Turn right and continue running on the paved path. (After this turn there is a parking area on the left and rest rooms on the right side of the trail.)

2.3 Turn right on the paved path as it skirts the right side of the picnic area.

2.4 Turn right on the paved path. (At this point you can jump onto the wood-chip jogging trail that parallels the paved path.)

2.5 Turn right at the trail junction and continue running on the wood-chip trail that parallels the paved path.

2.7 Turn left at the trail junction and continue cruising on the wood-chip trail that parallels the paved path.

2.9 Turn right and continue running on the wood-chip path that parallels the paved path.

3.0 Veer right and continue on the wood-chip path that parallels the paved path.

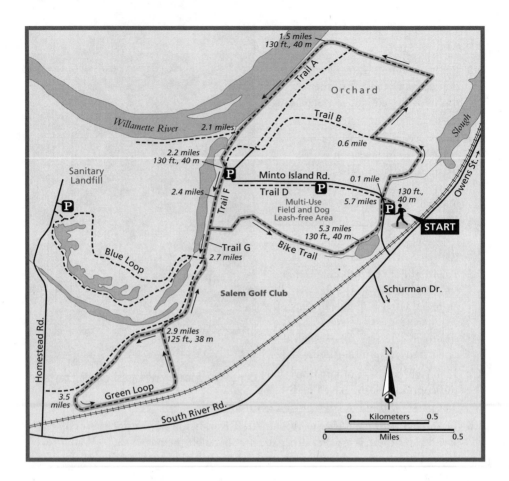

3.3 Continue straight (left). (A side trail heading right crosses a bridge.)

3.5 Turn left onto a dirt path. (The paved trail heads right at this junction.)

4.3 Turn right on the paved path and run on the wood-chip trail that parallels the paved path.

4.8 Turn right on the paved trail.

5.7 The paved path intersects with Minto Island Road. Cross the road and turn right onto the paved path on the other side.

5.8 Turn left into the parking area and the trailhead.

TRAIL FOOD

Willamette Brew Pub, 120 Commercial Street NE, Salem, OR 97301, (503) 363–9779

32: Silver Falls State Park Loop

Region/area:	Salem
Pain:	3
Gain:	4
Distance:	6.9-mile loop
Elevation gain:	515 feet
Time:	1.5 to 2 hours
The route:	This route takes you past many gorgeous waterfalls in Silver Falls State Park.
Trail surface:	85% smooth dirt, 10% rocky, 5% paved
Sun exposure:	30%
Runability:	100%
Season:	Year-round (the trail can be icy during the winter months)
Other users:	Hikers
Canine compatibility:	No dogs permitted
Permits/fees:	Oregon State Park $3.00 day-use fee
Trail contact:	Oregon State Parks and Recreation, Salem OR, (800) 551–6949, www.oregonstateparks.org/park_211.php
Maps:	USGS Drake Crossing (7.5' series); *Silver Falls State Park* trail map, available from Oregon State Parks, (800) 551–6949, www.oregonstateparks.org/images/pdf/silverfalls_trailmap.pdf

Trail scoop: This gorgeous singletrack path weaves through Silver Creek Canyon, past many spectacular waterfalls in Silver Falls State Park. The trail starts next to South Falls Lodge and descends steeply into the canyon. Immediately, you'll have a grand view of 177-foot South Falls—one of the park's most well known waterfalls. Before you know it the trail takes you behind the falls in a unique basalt cave. The cooling spray from the sweeping cascade is a welcome relief on a hot summer's day. The trail continues to travel along the South Fork of Silver Creek, through a forest of big-leaf maple, sword fern, and Douglas fir. After passing several unique water-falls, the trail follows the North Fork of Silver Creek and continues past more gorgeous canyon scenery. You'll finish the loop high up on the rim on the Ridge Trail, which takes you through more shady pine forest on a fast, smooth track. Your best trail-running experience will be during non–prime time tourist hours in the early spring or late fall. Rest rooms and water are available at the trailhead.

Scenic waterfall at Silver Falls State Park

Finding the trailhead: From I–5 in Salem turn east on Oregon Highway 22 toward North Santiam Highway–Stayton–Detroit Lake. Travel 5 miles east and take exit 7 onto Oregon Highway 214 toward Silver Falls State Park. At the end of the off-ramp, turn left onto Oregon 214 and continue 4.5 miles to a stop sign. Turn left at the stop sign and travel 12.2 miles on Oregon 214 to the entrance to Silver Falls State Park. After entering the park turn left at the South Falls turnoff. Proceed to the parking area and trailhead. *DeLorme: Oregon Atlas & Gazetteer:* Page 54 A3.

TRAIL DIRT

0.0 From the parking area begin running on a paved cobble path toward South Falls Lodge.

0.1 Turn left on the Canyon Trail as it descends steeply into Silver Creek Canyon. (As you descend you'll have a gorgeous view of 177-foot South Falls.)

0.2 Turn left and go behind the falls into a cool basalt cave.

0.3 Veer left and continue cruising along the well-traveled path. (The path turns to dirt at this junction.)

1.1 Admire 93-foot Lower South Falls.

1.4 Continue straight (left). (Ridge Trail heads right.)

2.4 Arrive at 30-foot Lower North Falls. Turn left and walk several yards to view 178-foot Double Falls.

2.5 Arrive at Double Falls. After viewing the falls turn around and head back to the main trail.

2.6 Turn left onto the main trail and cross a footbridge over Hult Creek.

2.8 Pass the short, fat cascade of Drake Falls.

3.0 Enjoy views of 103-foot Middle North Falls.

3.2 Continue straight (left). (The trail that heads right goes to Winter Falls.)

3.5 Pass 31-foot Twin Falls.

4.4 Arrive at your last waterfall on the route, 136-foot North Falls. Run behind the falls and then power up a steep set of concrete stairs that lead you to the canyon rim.

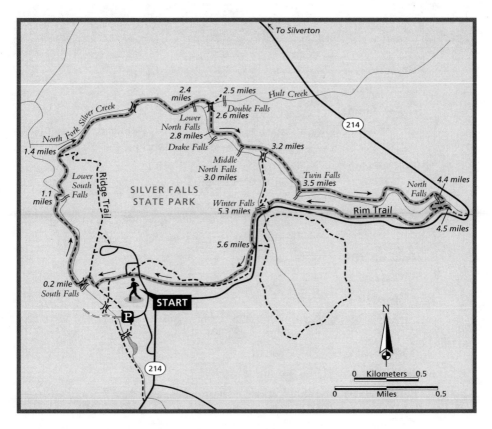

4.5 Turn sharply to the right and continue running on the Rim Trail.

5.3 Continue straight at the SOUTH FALLS TRAILHEAD 1.6 MILES sign. Run through a paved parking area and continue following the trail.

5.6 Turn right at the trail fork.

6.1 Turn right at the trail fork.

6.8 Cross a paved road.

6.9 Arrive at the trailhead parking area at South Falls.

TRAIL FOOD

Jonathan's Oyster Bar, 445 State Street, Salem, OR 97301, (503) 362–7219

33: Pamelia Lake

Region/area:	Salem
Pain:	2
Gain:	5
Distance:	4.4 miles out and back (with a 12.4-mile option to Hunts Cove and a 10.4-mile option to Grizzly Peak)
Elevation gain:	800 feet to Pamelia Lake; 2,150 feet to Hunts Cove; 2,700 feet to Grizzly Peak
Time:	50 minutes to 1 hour
The route:	This singletrack route travels through a magnificent old-growth forest to the shores of Pamelia Lake.
Trail surface:	100% smooth dirt
Sun exposure:	0%
Runability:	100%
Season:	May through November (Hunt's Cove and Grizzly Peak options: July through early November)
Other users:	Hikers, equestrians
Canine compatibility:	Dogs permitted
Permits/fees:	$5.00 Northwest Forest Pass, purchased by calling (800) 270–7504, or online at www.naturenw.org. *A special-use permit is required to access this trail.* You can obtain a permit at the Detroit Ranger Station. Call the ranger station at (503) 854–3366 for information.
Trail contact:	Detroit Ranger District, Mill City, OR, (503) 854–3366, www.fs.fed.us/r6/willamette
Maps:	USGS Mount Jefferson (7.5' series); Green Trails Mount Jefferson

Trail scoop: Take a step back in time when you run on this gorgeous singletrack trail through towering old-growth trees. Mossy-coated logs, wild rhododendrons, and picturesque Pamelia Creek are added bonuses to this near-perfect-10 trail—the only drawbacks are its popularity and having to deal with the hassle of getting a permit. After 2.2 miles you'll arrive at the inviting shores of Pamelia Lake. If you run this trail in the fall, you'll find more solitude and you'll get to enjoy the brilliant end-of-season colors. If you are in for a longer route, you may want to continue another 4 miles past Pamelia Lake on a steep uphill trek to scenic Hunts Cove, or you can continue 3 miles past the lake on a grueling climb to the summit of Grizzly Peak.

Finding the trailhead: Head 62 miles east of Salem on North Santiam Highway 22 to Pamelia Lake Road (Forest Service Road 2246). Turn left and travel 3.7 miles on Pamelia Lake Road to the parking area and trailhead. Rest rooms are available at the trailhead (no water). *DeLorme: Oregon Atlas & Gazetteer:* Page 56 C1.

TRAIL DIRT

0.0 Start your run on a wide forest path that takes you through an amazing old-growth forest.

2.2 Arrive at a trail intersection. Continue through this intersection toward the lakeshore and your turnaround point. From here, glide back down the same route to your

Fall foliage on the Pamelia Lake Trail

starting point. (**Options:** From the intersection at 2.2 miles, you have the option of continuing 4 miles to the secluded Hunts Cove. To get there, turn left and follow the trail as it winds around the left side of the lake. Ignore trails that peel off to the left toward the Pacific Crest Trail. Once you reach the other end

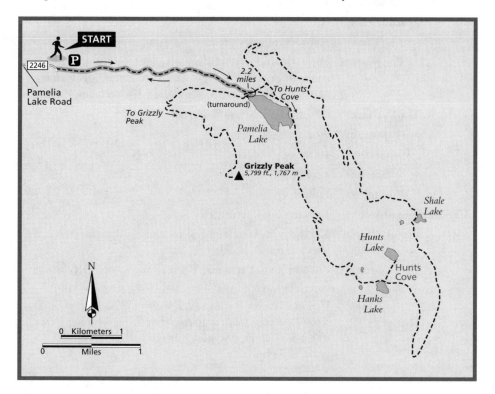

of the lake, continue on the trail to Hunts Cove, which you'll reach in 6.2 miles. Once you reach Hunts Cove, retrace your route back to your starting point, a run of 12.4 miles. Another trail option from the 2.2-mile intersection is to go right and continue 3 more steep miles to the summit of Grizzly Peak, where you'll have an incredible view of Mount Jefferson. Once you reach the summit, retrace the same route for a total mileage of 10.4.)

4.4 Arrive at the trailhead.

TRAIL FOOD

Indian Palace, 377 Court Street NE, Salem, OR 97301, (503) 371–4808

34: Willamette Mission State Park Loop

Region/area:	Salem
Pain:	1
Gain:	1
Distance:	2.3-mile loop
Elevation gain:	None
Time:	30 to 45 minutes
The route:	Dirt path and paved bike path that loop through filbert and walnut orchards, next to the Willamette River and Mission Lake and in Willamette Mission State Park.
Trail surface:	60% smooth dirt, 40% paved
Sun exposure:	90%
Runability:	100%
Season:	Year-round
Other users:	Hikers, cyclists
Canine compatibility:	Leashed dogs permitted
Permits/fees:	$3.00 day-use fee. You can purchase a day-use pass at the park's entrance booth.
Trail contact:	Oregon State Parks and Recreation, Salem, OR, (800) 551–6949, www.oregonstateparks.org/park_139.php
Maps:	USGS Mission Bottom (7.5' series); *Willamette Mission State Park* trail map, available from Oregon State Parks, (800) 551–6949, www.oregonstateparks.org/park_139.php

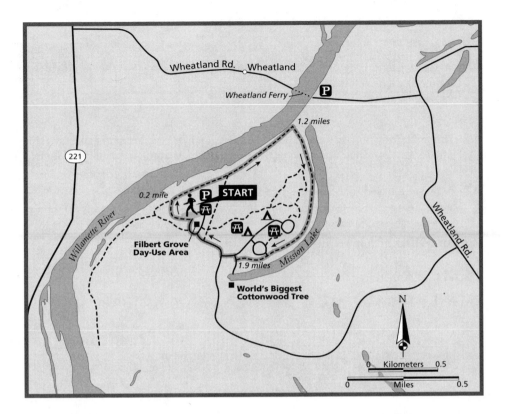

Trail scoop: This easy, serene route takes you on a tour past the scenic Willamette River, Mission Lake, and what is thought to be the world's biggest black cottonwood tree at 26 feet in circumference and 155 feet tall. You can follow the route cues for this fun loop or design your own route on the many trails in the park. Rest rooms and water are available at the trailhead.

Finding the trailhead: From I–5 take exit 263 toward Brooks and Gervais. (This exit is approximately 8 miles south of Woodburn and 9 miles north of Salem.) At the end of the off-ramp, set your mileage indicator to zero. Turn west onto Brooklake Road and go 1.6 miles to the intersection with Wheatland Road. Turn right onto Wheatland Road and drive 2.4 miles to the entrance road to Willamette Mission State Park. Turn left onto the park entrance road and drive 0.6 mile to the pay booth for the park. (You'll need to pay a $3.00 day-use fee. If an attendant is not in the pay booth, you can purchase a permit from the self-pay machine located at the entrance booth.) Continue 1.2 miles (staying to the left at each road junction) to the Filbert Grove Day-Use Area. *DeLorme: Oregon Atlas & Gazetteer:* Page 59 D8.

TRAIL DIRT

0.0 Start running on the trail adjacent to the rest rooms located at the far northwest corner of the parking area.

0.2 Turn right on the paved bike path that parallels the wide, lazy Willamette River.

1.2 Turn right on a grassy doubletrack road. Soon you'll pass Mission Lake on your left. As you continue through a walnut orchard, stay to the left at all trail junctions.

1.9 Arrive at a paved road and a signed road and a sign that points to the world's largest black cottonwood tree. Continue running on the paved road for 0.4 mile (at the first road junction, go left, and at the second road junction go right).

2.3 Arrive back at your starting point.

TRAIL FOOD

Great Harvest Bakery, 339 Court Street NE, Salem, OR 97301, (503) 363–4697

35: Dan's Trail

Region/area:	Corvallis
Pain:	3
Gain:	2
Distance:	8.2 miles out and back
Elevation gain:	780 feet
Time:	2 to 3 hours
The route:	This mostly singletrack route takes you to the top of 1,495-foot Dimple Hill in the McDonald Dunn Research Forest just outside of Corvallis. Views.
Trail surface:	80% smooth, 20% rocky
Sun exposure:	15%
Runability:	100%
Season:	Mid-April through October (closed from November through mid-April)
Other users:	Hikers, mountain bikers
Canine compatibility:	Leashed dogs permitted
Permits/fees:	None

Trail contact: Oregon State University, Corvallis, OR, (541) 737–6702 or (541) 737–4434 (recorded message), www.cof.orst.edu/resfor/rec/purpose.sht

Map: USGS Corvallis (7.5' series); you can obtain a map online at www.cof.orst.edu/resfor/rec/smcdfor.sht

Trail scoop: Just outside the Corvallis city limits is the McDonald Dunn Research Forest, which is host to dozens of trails that are very popular with runners, walkers, hikers, and mountain bikers. This out-and-back route gives you a good introduction to this fantastic trail-running area. The route starts in Chip Ross Park and climbs through scenic forest to the summit of 1,495-foot Dimple Hill. From the summit you'll have awesome views (on a clear day) of Corvallis and the surrounding Coast Mountain Range. Watch your footing on some nasty root sections.

Finding the trailhead: Head about 20 miles south of Salem on I–5 to exit 234B. At the end of the off-ramp, follow Pacific Boulevard Southeast for a mile until it turns into U.S. Highway 20. Continue following U.S. Highway 20 west toward Corvallis. After about 10 miles turn right onto Conifer Boulevard. Proceed 1.4 miles to State Highway 99 west. Turn left onto State Highway 99 west and go 0.3 mile to the intersection with Walnut Boulevard. Turn right onto Walnut Boulevard and travel 1.1 miles to Northwest Highland Drive. Turn right onto Northwest Highland Drive and proceed 0.9 mile to Lester Avenue. Turn left onto Lester Avenue and go 0.9 mile to the trailhead at the road's end at Chip Ross Park. *DeLorme: Oregon Atlas & Gazetteer:* Page 53 D6.

TRAIL DIRT

0.0 From the parking area, start running toward the yellow gate. Head north past the gate and continue on the old road that heads right. At the next trail fork head right. You'll immediately begin climbing. Ignore a trail on the left and then another on the right.

0.5 The trail levels off a bit. As you continue, ignore paths that head left off the main trail.

0.8 Turn right onto a singletrack trail and begin a fast downhill.

1.0 Arrive at a four-way intersection. Turn right and continue to the next trail intersection, where you'll head right on Dan's Trail.

1.1 Ignore the trail that heads left.

1.2 The route takes you under some ugly power lines. Ignore a trail that heads left as you begin a fast downhill.

1.6 Ignore a trail that heads right. At the next intersection, head left to continue your quest to reach the summit of Dimple Hill. Go across a gravel road and continue on Dan's Trail.

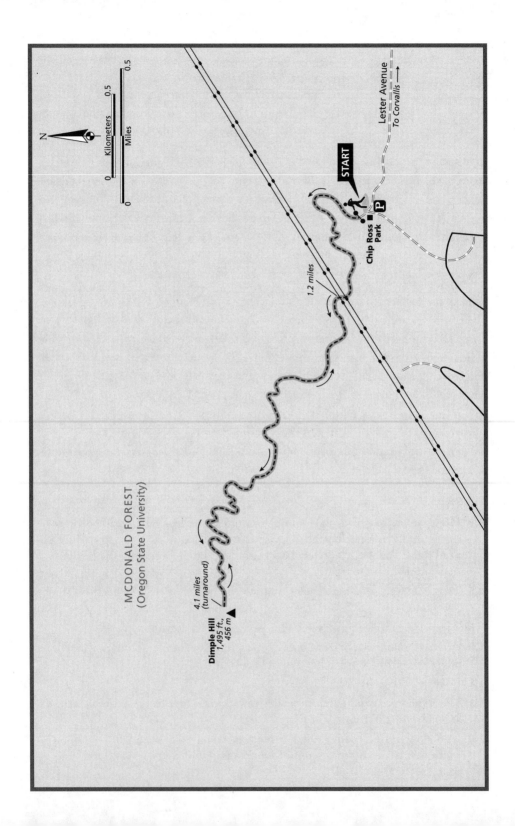

MCDONALD FOREST
(Oregon State University)

Dimple Hill
1,495 ft.,
456 m

4.1 miles
(turnaround)

1.2 miles

START

Chip Ross
Park

P

Lester Avenue
To Corvallis

N

Kilometers
0   0.5

Miles
0   0.5

2.1 Ignore a trail that heads left.

2.3 Arrive at the intersection with a doubletrack road. Continue to the left on the singletrack trail and get ready for some tough climbing.

2.8 Arrive at a four-way intersection. Continue straight and climb, climb, climb.

4.1 Arrive at the summit of 1,495-foot Dimple Hill, where the trail intersects with a gravel road. Enjoy the summit views and then retrace the same route back to the trailhead. *(Watch your speed on the descent and keep a sharp eye out for mountain bikers and hikers.)*

8.2 Arrive at the trailhead.

TRAIL FOOD

Mcmenamins–Corvallis, 420 Northwest 3rd Street, Corvallis, OR 97330, (541) 758–6044

36: Ridgeline Trail: Spencer Butte to Blanton Road

Region/area:	Eugene
Pain:	3
Gain:	3
Distance:	7.4 miles out and back
Elevation gain:	290 feet
Time:	1.5 to 2.5 hours
The route:	This urban singletrack route begins at Spencer Butte Park and heads on a blazing downhill through a scenic Douglas fir forest. The route heads northwest and crosses Willamette Street at mile 1.2. It continues along the ridgeline to the turnaround point at Blanton Road. Beware of the slick bridges on this route.
Trail surface:	90% smooth dirt, 10% rocky
Sun exposure:	10%
Runability:	100%
Season:	Year-round
Other users:	Hikers
Canine compatibility:	Leashed dogs permitted
Permits/fees:	None

Trail contact:	Eugene Parks, Eugene, OR, (541) 682–4800, www.ci.eugene.or.us/PW/PARKS/index.htm
Map:	USGS Creswell (7.5' series)

Trail scoop: This route takes you on a fun journey through an enchanting forest right in the heart of Eugene. The trail teases you by heading downhill for the first half and saving the tough uphill for the finish. This trail can be a mud fest during the winter months.

Finding the trailhead: From the intersection of 7th and Willamette Streets in downtown Eugene, turn south onto Willamette Street and travel 5.3 miles to Spencer Butte Park on the left side of the road. Look carefully for the small park sign indicating the entrance to the park—it's easy to miss! A rest room is available at the trailhead (no water). *DeLorme: Oregon Atlas & Gazetteer:* Page 47 D8.

TRAIL DIRT

0.0 From the parking area go around a set of yellow metal posts and proceed on the middle trail.

0.5 Turn right at a three-way intersection.

1.2 Turn left at a three-way intersection. Continue blasting downhill on a series of tight switchbacks.

1.3 Cross a wooden bridge that can be slick!

2.2 Arrive at a gravel parking area under a set of power lines. Head across the parking lot and then cross South Willamette Street. Turn right and run parallel to South Willamette Street for about 300 yards until you see a sign marking the continuation of the Ridgeline Trail. Turn left at the trail sign and continue on the singletrack trail as it sails along the ridgeline through a shady forest.

3.7 Arrive at a gravel parking area at Blanton Road. From here, turnaround and retrace the route back to the trailhead at Spencer Butte.

7.4 Arrive at the trailhead.

TRAIL FOOD

Keystone Café, 395 West 5th Avenue, Eugene, OR 97401, (541) 342–2075
Steelhead Brewery, 188 East 5th Avenue, Eugene, OR 97401, (541) 686–2739

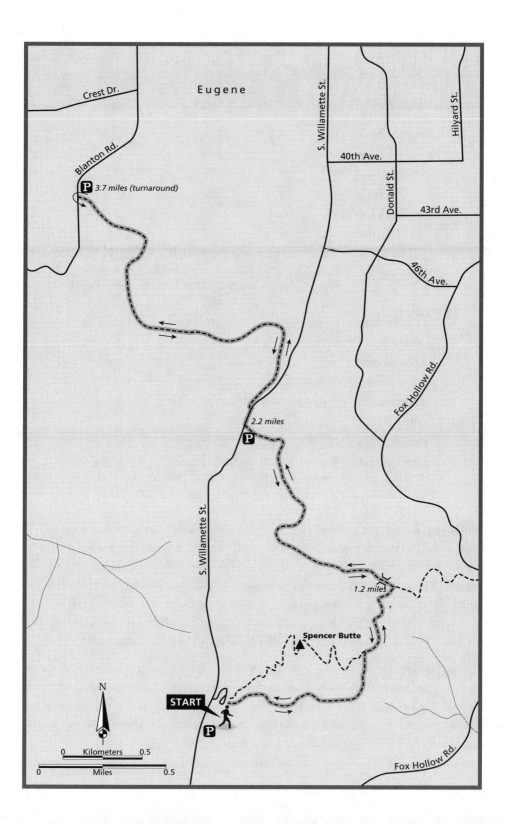

Crest Dr.

E u g e n e

S. Willamette St.

Hilyard St.

Blanton Rd.

40th Ave.

Donald St.

43rd Ave.

P *3.7 miles (turnaround)*

46th Ave.

Fox Hollow Rd.

2.2 miles

P

S. Willamette St.

1.2 miles

Spencer Butte

START

P

N

0   Kilometers   0.5

0   Miles   0.5

Fox Hollow Rd.

37: Ridgeline Trail Loop: Spencer Butte to Fox Hollow Road

Region/Area:	Eugene
Pain:	3
Gain:	3
Distance:	7-mile loop
Elevation gain:	250 feet
Time:	1.25 to 2 hours
The route:	This route begins at the base of Spencer Butte, follows Ridgeline Trail across Fox Hollow Road, completes a loop, and then heads back to Spencer Butte Park. Slippery wooden ramps.
Trail surface:	90% smooth dirt, 10% rocky
Sun exposure:	10%
Runability:	100%
Season:	Year-round
Other users:	Hikers, mountain bikers
Canine compatibility:	Leashed dogs permitted
Permits/fees:	None
Trail contact:	Eugene Parks, Eugene, OR, (541) 682–4800, www.ci.eugene.or.us/PW/PARKS/index.htm
Map:	USGS Creswell (7.5' series)

Trail scoop: Escape the city and clear your lungs on a hilly section of the scenic Ridgeline Trail that begins at Spencer Butte Park. Cruise through deep forest with pockets of magnificent old-growth fir—just don't wipe out on the slick wooden bridges! The route heads down steep switchbacks and then crosses Fox Hollow Road. After the road crossing you'll complete a quiet forest loop where you'll be sharing part of the trail with mountain bikers. After completing the loop the route promises a good workout when you crank back uphill to your starting point.

Finding the trailhead: From the intersection of 7th and Willamette Streets in downtown Eugene, turn south on Willamette Street and travel 5.3 miles to Spencer Butte Park on the left side of the road. Look carefully for the small park sign indicating the entrance to the park—it is easy to miss! A rest room is available at the trailhead (no water). *DeLorme: Oregon Atlas & Gazetteer:* Page 47 D8.

TRAIL DIRT

0.0 From parking area go around a set of yellow metal posts and proceed on the middle trail.

0.5 Turn right at a three-way intersection.

1.2 Arrive at a three-way intersection. Turn right toward Fox Hollow Road. A sign states you'll arrive at Fox Hollow Road in 0.7 mile.

1.9 Cross Fox Hollow Road. After crossing the road turn right and follow the guardrail that parallels the road for about 50 yards. Then turn left and continue on the unsigned singletrack trail. Continue on the trail for about 100 yards and arrive at a small gravel parking lot. Traverse the parking lot and continue on the singletrack trail on the opposite side. Go another 25 yards to a trail fork. Head right and begin cranking uphill.

Afternoon run on the Ridgeline Trail

2.7 Turn left at a trail fork. Continue 50 yards and then continue straight downhill. (At this point you are on the signed mountain-bike portion of the trail.)

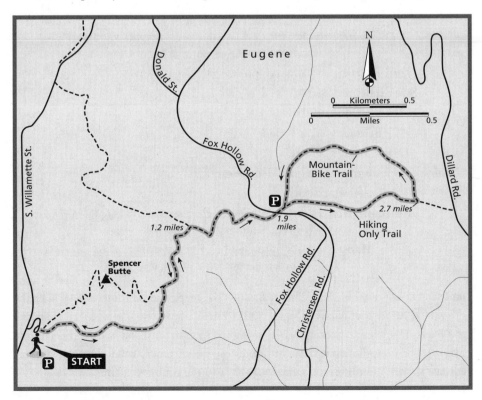

3.4 Continue straight (left). (Ignore a side trail that drops sharply to the right.)

3.5 The loop portion of the route ends. Retrace the same route back to your starting point.

7.0 Arrive at the trailhead.

TRAIL FOOD

Keystone Café, 395 West 5th Avenue, Eugene, OR 97401, (541) 342–2075

Steelhead Brewery, 188 East 5th Avenue, Eugene, OR 97401, (541) 686–2739

38: Mount Pisgah Summit

Region/area:	Eugene
Pain:	4
Gain:	2
Distance:	3-mile loop
Elevation gain:	990 feet
Time:	45 minutes to 1.25 hours
The route:	This wide gravel path climbs relentlessly through oak woodlands to the summit of Mount Pisgah. Views.
Trail surface:	65% smooth dirt, 35% rocky
Sun exposure:	80%
Runability:	100%
Season:	Year-round
Other users:	Hikers
Canine compatibility:	Leashed dogs permitted
Permits/fees:	None
Trail contact:	Lane County Parks, Eugene, OR, (541) 682–4414, www.co.lane.or.us/parks/laneParks.htm
Maps:	USGS Springfield (7.5' series); *Howard Buford Recreation Area* brochure, available at the trailhead

Trail scoop: Just outside Eugene's city limits, this steep, intense route takes you to the summit of 1,516-foot Mount Pisgah. This route is not for the average trail runner—you have to truly enjoy searing cardio workouts to take on this beast. At the summit a bronze marker points out views of distant mountain peaks. You'll return on a blazing fast downhill dash on the same route back to the trailhead. (Your knees may

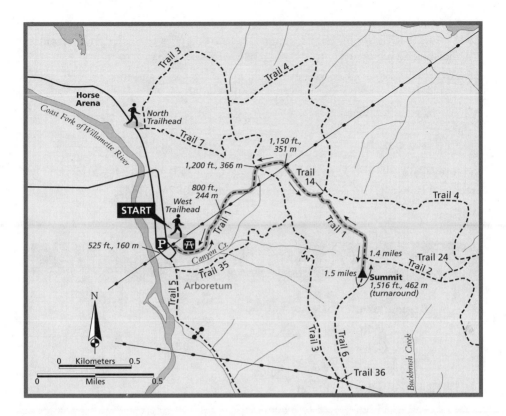

appreciate a gentle lope down the steeper grades.) No water is available at the trail-head.

Finding the trailhead: From I–5 at the edge of Eugene's southern city limits, take exit 189, 30th Avenue–South Eugene. At the end of the off-ramp, continue straight for 0.2 mile. Turn right onto Franklin Avenue (a Texaco Station is on the corner) and go 0.4 mile to the intersection with Seavey Loop Road. Turn left onto Seavey Loop Road and travel 1.5 miles and cross a bridge that takes you over the Coast Fork of the Willamette River. After crossing the bridge continue 0.4 mile on a gravel road to a large gravel parking area and the trailhead. *DeLorme: Oregon Atlas & Gazetteer: Page 48 D1.*

TRAIL DIRT

0.0 Start by going around a brown metal gate on the east side of the parking lot. Start running on the #1 trail located next to the brown trail sign. (This wide gravel trail immediately starts its steep climb through oak woodlands and meadows to the summit of Mount Pisgah.)

1.0 Continue straight on Trail #1. (The North Boundary Trail #4 joins Trail #1 from the left.)

1.4 Continue straight on Trail #1 (ignore Trail #2 that goes to the left). (The grade mellows, giving your numb arms and blurred vision a chance to recover.)

1.5 Arrive at the summit of Mount Pisgah. Enjoy the views and then turn around and blast downhill on the same route to the trailhead.

3.0 Arrive at the trailhead.

TRAIL FOOD

Keystone Café, 395 West 5th Avenue, Eugene, OR 97401, (541) 342–2075
Steelhead Brewery, 188 East 5th Avenue, Eugene, OR 97401, (541) 686–2739

39: Mount Pisgah Arboretum Loop

Region/area:	Eugene
Pain:	3
Gain:	3
Distance:	4.7-mile loop
Elevation gain:	700 feet
Time:	1.25 to 2 hours
The route:	This loop route begins in the Mount Pisgah Arboretum and takes you on a journey through oak woodlands, open meadows, and cool evergreen forest.
Trail surface:	60% smooth dirt, 40% rocky
Sun exposure:	65%
Runability:	100%
Season:	Year-round
Other users:	Hikers, equestrians
Canine compatibility:	Leashed dogs permitted
Permits/fees:	None
Trail contact:	Lane County Parks, Eugene, OR, (541) 682–4414, www.co.lane.or.us/parks/laneParks.htm
Maps:	USGS Springfield (7.5' series); *Howard Buford Recreation Area* brochure, available at the trailhead

Trail scoop: This loop route takes you through the many different landscapes of the Mount Pisgah Arboretum. There are some subtle trail junctions and certain parts of the route you'll possibly share with horses. No water is available at the trailhead.

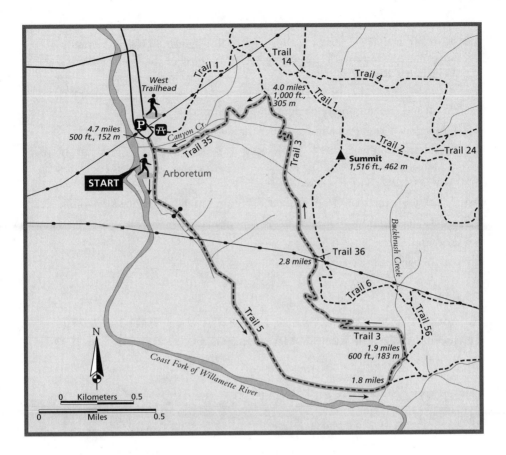

Finding the trailhead: From I–5 at the edge of Eugene's southern city limits, take exit 189, 30th–South Eugene. At the end of the off-ramp, continue straight for 0.2 mile. Turn right onto Franklin Avenue (a Texaco Station is on the corner) and go 0.4 mile to the intersection with Seavey Loop Road. Turn left onto Seavey Loop Road and travel 1.5 miles and cross a bridge that takes you over the Coast Fork of the Willamette River. After crossing the bridge continue 0.4 mile on a gravel road to large gravel parking area. Proceed through the main parking area until you reach another parking area at the signed Mount Pisgah Arboretum. *DeLorme: Oregon Atlas & Gazetteer:* Page 48 D1.

TRAIL DIRT

0.0 From the Arboretum parking area, start running on the signed Riverbank Trail.

0.3 Turn left onto Quarry Road.

0.5 Go around a metal gate and continue straight.

0.8 The trail turns to grassy singletrack.

1.8 Turn left at the trail fork, which is hard to distinguish. (This trail junction appears a few hundred yards after your last glimpse of the Coast Fork of the Willamette River.)

1.9 Ignore the faint trail that heads off to the right. At this point the trail heads uphill and becomes more obvious and a bit rutted.

2.8 Cross gravel Trail #36 and continue straight under a set of power lines.

4.0 Turn left onto the signed #35 connector trail. A sign reads WEST TRAILHEAD 0.7 MILE. *(Watch your footing on this technical downhill section—it has sections of rocks that can be slick if it's wet out.)*

4.4 A trail joins the route from the left. Continue straight and head downhill.

4.5 Continue straight (ignoring the trail that heads right).

4.6 Veer right.

4.7 Arrive back at the trailhead.

TRAIL FOOD

Keystone Café, 395 West 5th Avenue, Eugene, OR 97401, (541) 342–2075
Steelhead Brewery, 188 East 5th Avenue, Eugene, OR 97401, (541) 686–2739

40: Salmon Creek

Region/area:	Oakridge
Pain:	2
Gain:	3
Distance:	7.6 miles out and back
Elevation gain:	140 feet
Time:	1.25 to 1.50 hours
The route:	An inspiring singletrack and doubletrack route that races along scenic Salmon Creek.
Trail surface:	95% smooth dirt, 5% rocky
Sun exposure:	5%
Runability:	100%
Season:	Year-round
Other users:	Mountain bikers, hikers
Canine compatibility:	Dogs permitted
Permits/fees:	None

Smooth sailing on the Salmon Creek Trail

Trail contact:	Middle Fork Ranger District, Lowell, OR, (541) 937–2129, www.fs.fed.us/r6/willamette
Map:	USGS Oakridge and Westfir East (7.5' series)

Trail scoop: You'll love this fast, easy route that sweeps through attractive forest along the banks of cheery Salmon Creek. If you are treading trail during school hours, you'll likely see the local high-school cross-country team in action. This fun forest route is green and cool in the summer and golden in the fall. As an added bonus you'll get to check out a picturesque wood bridge that spans the creek at your turn-around point. Watch out for warp-speed mountain bikers on this fast dirt track. No rest rooms or water are available at the trailhead.

Finding the trailhead: From I–5 in Eugene take exit 188A, Highway 58/Oakridge/Klamath Falls. Head east on Highway 58 for about 36 miles to Oakridge. From the bridge crossing Salmon Creek in Oakridge, travel 1.2 miles east on Highway 58 to Fish Hatchery Road. Turn left onto Fish Hatchery Road, go 1.3 miles and turn right onto an obscure dirt lane that takes you to the trailhead. (You'll reach this turnoff area immediately after you cross a bridge over Salmon Creek.) *DeLorme: Oregon Atlas & Gazetteer:* Page 43 B5.

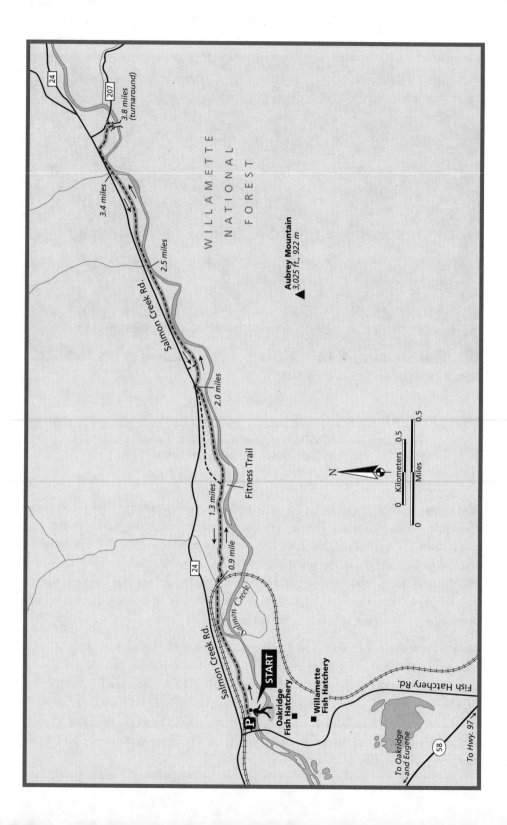

24

207

3.8 miles
(turnaround)

3.4 miles

2.5 miles

Salmon Creek Rd.

2.0 miles

WILLAMETTE
NATIONAL
FOREST

Aubrey Mountain
3,025 ft., 922 m

1.3 miles

Fitness Trail

0.9 mile

N

0   Kilometers   0.5
0   Miles   0.5

24

Salmon Creek

Salmon Creek Rd.

START

P

Oakridge
Fish Hatchery

Willamette
Fish Hatchery

Fish Hatchery Rd.

To Oakridge
and Eugene

58

To Hwy. 97

TRAIL DIRT

0.0 Start on the dirt path, which quickly takes you on a short downhill and crosses a wood bridge. The path then widens and winds through a shady canopy of Douglas fir and big-leaf maple. (It is virtually impossible to get lost on this route because it's bordered by Salmon Creek Road on one side and Salmon Creek on the other side.)

0.1 Veer left.

0.4 Keep zipping along on the trail and ignore a doubletrack road that heads left.

0.9 Go underneath a train trestle.

1.0 Continue straight on the main trail and ignore a spur trail that heads left.

1.3 Turn right onto the signed Fitness Trail.

2.0 Cross a doubletrack road and continue straight on the singletrack trail.

2.1 Turn right at the trail junction.

2.5 The trail narrows on a steep bank above the creek. Ignore a spur trail that heads left toward a paved road.

2.6 The trail turns into a doubletrack road. Go 200 yards and arrive at a road junction. Continue straight and ignore the doubletrack road that peels off to the right.

3.3 Turn left at the trail junction. (The trail that goes right dead-ends at a primitive campsite.) Go another 30 feet and then take a sharp right onto an unmarked singletrack trail.

3.4 The trail intersects with paved Salmon Creek Road. Turn right and run on the dirt trail next to Salmon Creek Road.

3.6 Turn right onto the signed Salmon Creek Trail #4365.

3.7 Turn right on a doubletrack road and follow this road 0.1 mile to a primitive camping area. Continue toward the creek and pick up a singletrack trail.

3.8 Arrive at a picturesque wood bridge spanning Salmon Creek (your turnaround point). Retrace the same route back to your starting point.

7.6 Arrive back at the trailhead.

TRAIL FOOD

Timber Jim's Pizza, 47527 Highway 58, Oakridge, OR 97463, (541) 782–4310

Region/area:	Oakridge
Pain:	4
Gain:	4
Distance:	10.2 miles out and back
Elevation gain:	700 feet
Time:	3 to 4 hours
The route:	This technical singletrack route passes through a magnificent old-growth forest next to mossy Larison Creek in the Willamette National Forest. Bridgeless creek crossings.
Trail surface:	65% smooth dirt, 35% rocky
Sun exposure:	5%
Runability:	95%
Season:	May to October
Other users:	Mountain bikers, hikers
Canine compatibility:	Dogs permitted
Permits/fees:	$5.00 Northwest Forest Pass, purchased by calling (800) 270–7504, or online at www.naturenw.org.
Trail contact:	Middle Fork Ranger District, Lowell, OR, (541) 937–2129, www.fs.fed.us/r6/willamette
Map:	USGS Oakridge and Holland Point (7.5' series)

Trail scoop: Have a day filled with adventure on this old-growth trail that sweeps up Larison Creek canyon. Mossy-coated logs, trees, and rocks create a glistening green canvas, and the soothing sounds of the creek make you want the trail to never end. This trail will challenge you with its many sections of roots, rocks, and creek crossings. Also beware of mountain bikers, who love the challenge of riding this technical trail. No rest rooms or water are available at the trailhead.

Finding the trailhead: From I–5 in Eugene take exit 188A, Highway 58/Oakridge/Klamath Falls. Head east on Highway 58 for about 36 miles to Oakridge. From the bridge crossing Salmon Creek in Oakridge, travel 1.4 miles east on Highway 58 to Kitson Springs Road (Forest Service Road 23) at the HILLS CREEK DAM sign. Turn right onto Kitson Springs Road and travel 0.5 mile to Diamond Drive (Forest Service Road 21). Turn right onto Diamond Drive and go 2.4 miles to a dirt parking lot and trailhead on the right side of the road. The trailhead is marked with a brown hiker sign. *DeLorme: Oregon Atlas & Gazetteer:* Page 43 C5.

The beautiful Larison Creek Trail

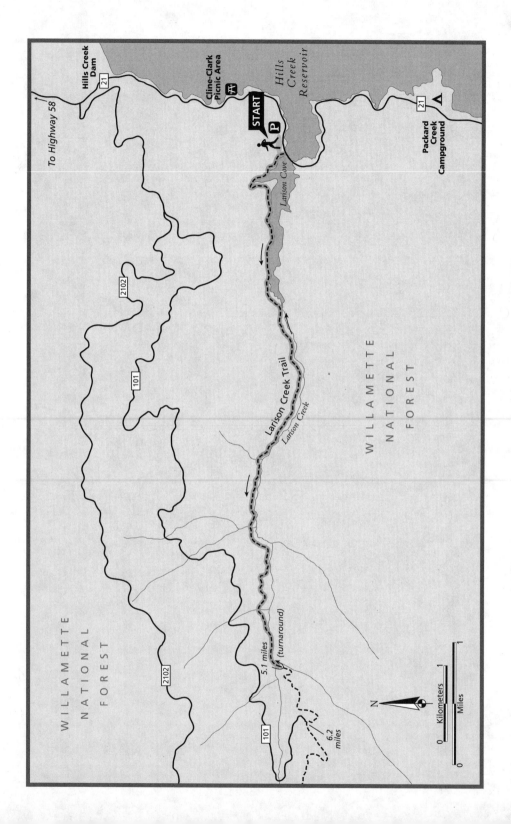

WILLAMETTE NATIONAL FOREST

To Highway 58

Hills Creek Dam

21

Cline-Clark Picnic Area

START

P

Hills Creek Reservoir

Larison Cove

21

Packard Creek Campground

2102

101

Larison Creek Trail

Larison Creek

WILLAMETTE NATIONAL FOREST

2102

101

5.1 miles (turnaround)

6.2 miles

N

0   1   Kilometers

0   1   Miles

TRAIL DIRT

0.0 Start running on the singletrack Larison Creek Trail.

0.5 Pass a rest room on your left. Go 50 yards and cross a wood bridge over the creek and pass a campsite on your right.

3.1 You'll have to negotiate a bridgeless creek crossing.

5.1 Arrive at the turnaround point at a bridgeless creek crossing with a huge wood log spanning the creek. From this point reverse the trail directions back to your starting point. (**Option:** You have the option of crossing the creek and continuing another 1.1 miles to the end of the trail at 6.2 miles. However, this is not recommended because the trail is very steep and passes through an ugly, overgrown clear-cut the last 0.5 mile.)

10.2 Arrive at the trailhead.

TRAIL FOOD

High Lakes Café, 47434 Highway 58, Oakridge, OR 97463, (541) 782–2486

42: McKenzie River

Region/area:	Eugene
Pain:	1
Gain:	4
Distance:	5 miles out and back (26.5-mile shuttle option)
Elevation gain:	170 feet (1,800 feet for the 26.5-mile route)
Time:	45 minutes to 1 hour
The route:	Outstanding singletrack route that travels through an old-growth forest along the banks of the McKenzie River in the Willamette National Forest.
Trail surface:	100% smooth dirt
Sun exposure:	5%
Runability:	100%
Season:	April through November
Other users:	Hikers, mountain bikers
Canine compatibility:	Dogs permitted
Permits/fees:	None

Running through old growth giants on the McKenzie River Trail

Trail contact:	Willamette National Forest, McKenzie Ranger District, McKenzie Bridge, OR, (541) 822–3381, www.fs.fed.us/r6/willamette
Map:	USGS McKenzie Bridge, Tamolitch Falls, Clear Lake (7.5' series)

Trail scoop: Here is your chance to run next to one of the best river trails in the West! This route will dazzle you with its wide smooth track, gorgeous old-growth trees, and crystal-clear river. The trail weaves in and out of magical forest and at several different points takes you near the river's edge until you reach Paradise Campground—your turnaround point. If you're amped for more river running, the trail continues upriver for 24 more gorgeous miles! Ultra trail-running fans can compete in the McKenzie River 50K Trail Run, held on this route in September. No rest rooms or water are available at the trailhead.

Finding the trailhead: Head 51 miles east of Eugene on Oregon Highway 126. Turn left into the trailhead parking area just before milepost 52. **(Shuttle option:** If you want to complete the entire 26.5-mile trail as a bike or car shuttle, continue another 25.5 miles east on Oregon Highway 126 to the intersection with a dirt road. Turn right and follow signs to the McKenzie River Trailhead.) *DeLorme: Oregon Atlas & Gazetteer:* Page 49 C6.

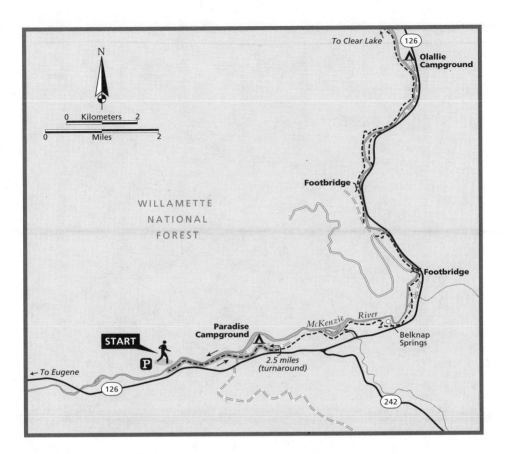

TRAIL DIRT

0.0 From the parking area, head east on the McKenzie River Trail.

1.4 Cross a dirt road and continue cruising on the smooth McKenzie River Trail.

2.5 Arrive at the paved entrance road to Paradise Campground (your turnaround point). From here, retrace the same route back to your starting point. (**Option:** You can continue for another 24 miles on this awesome river trail.)

5.0 Arrive back at the trailhead.

TRAIL FOOD

Log Cabin Inn Restaurant, 56483 McKenzie Highway, Blue River, OR 97413, (541) 822–3432

Rustic Skillet, 54771 McKenzie Highway, Blue River, OR 97413, (541) 822–3400

Central Oregon

D ry and sunny weather welcomes trail runners in the central part of Oregon. This area features a high desert ecosystem of sagebrush, juniper, and ponderosa pine, amazing gorges, and unique rock formations that reflect this area's volcanic past. Coursing through all this is the Deschutes River, beginning high in the Cascade Mountains and traveling north to south through the heart of Bend, Central Oregon's largest city. Bend has dozens of quality trails within minutes of downtown. Located at an elevation of 3,600 feet at the foot of the Central Cascade Mountains, Bend is an outdoor lover's paradise with trail running at the top of the list. Eight major peaks between 7,800 and 10,500 feet dominate its Western horizon, including Mount Bachelor, Broken Top, North, Middle and South Sister, Mount Washington, Three Fingered Jack, and Mount Jefferson. The Three Sisters Wilderness and Deschutes National Forest are located right out the back door, and the moody Deschutes River flows right through Drake Park in the center of downtown.

The Cascade Lakes Highway heads west out of town and is the main arterial to some of the classic running trails in this part of Oregon. You can coast on the beautiful Deschutes River Trail or climb up to the Green Lakes Basin in the Three Sisters Wilderness on the Green Lakes Loop Trail. Another popular city trail is First Street Rapids, which parallels the Deschutes River on the northwest side of town. You can truly experience the volcanic intensity of this part of the state by running on the Paulina Lake Trail. This loop trail takes you around the shores of Paulina Lake past lava flows and piles of shiny black obsidian located in the Newberry National Volcanic Monument.

If you travel 30 miles northwest of Bend on U.S. Highway 20, you'll reach the small western-style town of Sisters. Sisters is surrounded by an open, sunny ponderosa pine forest, dramatic volcanic peaks, and the wild and scenic Metolius River. The Three Sisters Mountains stand as sentinels to the west with 6,436-foot Black Butte—one of the state's tallest cinder cones—brooding in the forefront. If you want to climb to the top of this brooding mountain, take a spin on the Black Butte Summit Trail. If mountains are your mantra, be sure to test your quads on the Tam McArthur Rim Trail, which takes you to the top of a dramatic windswept ridge with unsurpassed views of the Central Cascade range and the Three Creeks Lake Basin. If you love river runs, you don't want to miss the West Metolius River Trail, which saunters along the crystal-clear waters of wild and scenic Metolius River.

A spectacular high-desert route you should check out is the Smith Rock State Park Trail, located 6 miles northeast of Redmond and 21 miles northeast of Bend off U.S. Highway 97. This route takes you through a striking sage and juniper landscape into the dramatic Crooked River Canyon surrounded by 400-foot-high cliffs.

43: Smith Rock State Park Loop

Region/area:	Redmond
Pain:	4
Gain:	5
Distance:	4-mile loop
Elevation gain:	700 feet
Time:	1.25 to 1.75 hours
The route:	Dirt trail that explores the spectacular Crooked River Canyon and then climbs to the summit of Misery Ridge. Mountain views. Bridge crossings.
Trail surface:	60% smooth dirt, 40% rocky
Sun exposure:	100%
Runability:	90%
Season:	Year-round
Other users:	Hikers, mountain bikers, equestrians
Canine compatibility:	Leashed dogs permitted
Permits/fees:	$3.00 state park pass fee required. You can purchase a day-use permit from the self-pay station in the main parking area.
Trail contact:	Oregon State Parks and Recreation, Salem OR, (800) 551–6949, www.oregonstateparks.org/park_51.php
Maps:	USGS Redmond (7.5' series); *Smith Rock State Park* trail map, available from Oregon State Parks, (800) 551–6949, or online at www.oregonstateparks.org/park_51.php

Trail scoop: Cruise through a desert canyon along the meandering Crooked River and towering volcanic spires. Initially it's hard to concentrate on the trail with its myriad of distractions. World-class climbing, beautiful canyon scenery, and gawking tourists will test your trail navigation skills. Soon enough you'll escape this scene and head into the tranquil lower canyon. After a couple miles of blissful trail, you'll arrive at Monkey Face—an awesome pillar with the likeness of a grinning monkey. Shift into your granny gear and head up mega-steep switchbacks to the ridge crest. Soak up grand views from the top of prominent Central Cascade volcanoes as your body recovers. Check your brakes and head down the Misery Ridge Trail to the canyon floor. You'll finish this spectacular loop by trekking along the canyon floor and then heading back to your starting point. The sun can be brutal on this trail and water is a must. Water and rest rooms are available at the trailhead.

Dramatic Smith Rock State Park

Finding the trailhead: From Redmond travel 5 miles north on U.S. Highway 97 to the small town of Terrebonne. At the flashing yellow light, turn right onto B Avenue (this turns into Smith Rock Way after the first stop sign). Continue 3.3 miles northeast, following the signs to Smith Rock State Park. *DeLorme: Oregon Atlas & Gazetteer:* Page 51 B7.

TRAIL DIRT

0.0 From the parking area head toward the canyon and take a right on an asphalt trail. Follow this to the canyon rim, where it begins its rough and raggedy spiral into Crooked River Canyon. After about 50 yards of careful descent, turn right onto a foot trail. Shuffle down this steep and slick trail to the canyon floor.

0.4 Cross a footbridge over the Crooked River. After you cross the bridge, turn left where a sign states Morning Glory wall is 0.25 mile, and Monkey Face is 1.5 miles. Set your legs free on this section while checking out the gorgeous scenery and rock-climbing action.

1.6 Turn right at a trail fork near the base of Monkey Face. (This amazing pillar is host to some of the most difficult rock climbs in the world.) From this intersection you'll power up killer switchbacks to the top of the ridge. The trail forks near the top, veer right and continue your ascent.

2.1 Arrive at the top of the ridge. Once you reach the top be on the lookout for wood trail markers that are signed P for the parking area. There are many side trails that spin off the route at the top of the ridge. Stay on the main trail and be on the lookout for the trail markers. (While you are at it, look to the west to view several prominent Cascade volcanoes, including Mount Bachelor, North Sister, Middle Sister, South Sister, Mount Washington, Mount Jefferson, and, to the far north, Mount Hood.) Continue along the ridge for 0.2 mile until you begin descending on a very steep, loose trail known as Misery Ridge. *(Watch your footing on this hill as you head down switchbacks and multiple stairs.)*

3.0 Arrive at the canyon floor. Continue straight and cross a footbridge over the Crooked River. The trail forks after the bridge; turn right and run on the wide dirt track that parallels the river.

High desert running at its best at Smith Rock State Park

3.1 Turn right onto a smaller foot trail as the main trail switchbacks left up the hill. Continue running through a burn area dating from the mid-1990s.

3.4 Turn left at the base of a large basalt rock called Rope De Dope block. Begin climbing stairs to the left side of this rock. At the next trail junction, veer left and continue climbing to the top of the ridge.

3.8 Arrive at the top of the ridge and a trail junction. Turn left onto a gravel trail that parallels the edge of the rim and offers awesome views in every direction of the park and Crooked River Canyon. After about 50 yards turn left onto the path that leads back to the main parking area and the trailhead.

4.0 Arrive at the trailhead.

Smith Rock Geology

The park's jagged cliffs are remnants of ash deposits from ancient volcanoes. Gray Butte Complex, of which these volcanoes are a part, is made up of several different volcanic rock types that originate from the Miocene period nearly 17 to 19 million years ago. A variety of surfaces and textures have formed to create rough-faced cliffs and dihedrals that attract climbers worldwide.

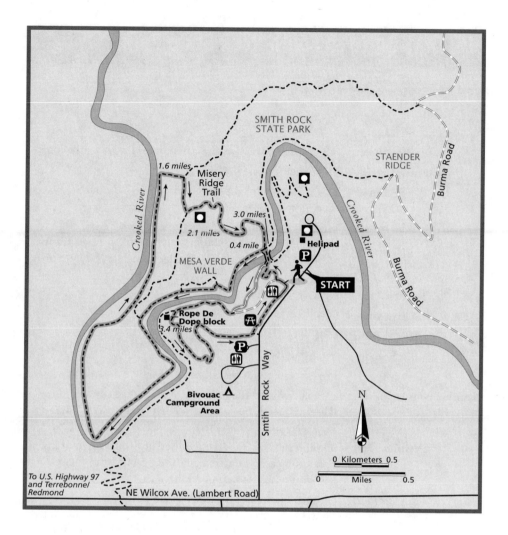

TRAIL FOOD

Abby's Legendary Pizza, 413 Southwest Glacier Avenue, Redmond, OR 97756,
(541) 548–5266

Cisco & Panchos, 343 Northwest 6th Street, Redmond, OR 97756, (541)
923–5042

La Siesta, 8320 North Highway 97, Terrebonne, OR 97760, (541) 548–4848

44: Gray Butte to Smith Rock State Park

Region/area:	Redmond
Pain:	5
Gain:	4
Distance:	8.8 miles one way (with a car shuttle) or 17.6-mile loop
Elevation gain:	1,540 feet
Time:	2 to 2.5 hours for 8.8-mile route or 5 to 7 hours for 17.6-mile loop
The route:	High-desert trail that skirts the northwest edge of Gray Butte and then takes you into the Crooked River Canyon at Smith Rock State Park. Bridge crossings. Mountain views.
Trail surface:	65% smooth dirt, 35% rocky
Sun exposure:	100%
Runability:	95%
Season:	Year-round
Other users:	Hikers, mountain bikers, equestrians
Canine compatibility:	Dogs permitted (dogs can be under voice command on BLM property, but once you enter Smith Rock State Park they must be leashed)
Permits/fees:	$3.00 state park pass fee required at Smith Rock State Park. You can purchase a day-use permit from the self-pay station in the main parking area.
Trail contact:	Ochoco National Forest, Crooked River National Grassland, Madras, OR, (541) 475–9272, www.fs.fed.us/r6/centraloregon/; Oregon State Parks and Recreation, Salem, OR, (800) 551–6949, www.oregonstateparks.org/park_51.php
Map:	USGS Redmond and Gray Butte (7.5' series)

Trail scoop: If you love deserts and solitude, this run is for you. This singletrack route skirts the northwest edge of 5,108-foot Gray Butte, located in the high-desert landscape of Crooked River National Grassland and ending at Smith Rock State Park. The trail weaves its way through a sage- and juniper-scented landscape around the base of Gray Butte. It then clings to the edge of two prominent ridges, offering awesome views of the Three Sisters volcanoes, Broken Top, Black Butte, and Mount Jefferson. After 6.2 miles you'll enter the volcanic landscape of Smith Rock State Park. This 641-acre park features a beautiful canyon carved by the Crooked River.

Cruising on the Gray Butte Trail

Dramatic rock spires are the backdrop to this rugged landscape. Over the next 4 miles, you'll descend to the bottom of the canyon and run next to the meandering Crooked River, which is home to Canadian geese, ducks, and river otter. You'll end this spectacular run at the Smith Rock State Park main parking area located on the canyon rim. Adjacent to the parking area is a shady picnic area that has rest rooms and water. Unless you are training for an ultramarathon, it is recommend that you complete this run with a car or bike shuttle. If you are completing this route as a loop, be sure to stock up on water before you head back because no water is available at the trailhead. There aren't any rest rooms at the trailhead either, but they are available at Smith Rock State Park.

Finding the trailhead: If you want to complete this run with a car or bike shuttle, leave your transportation at Smith Rock State Park. To get to the Smith Rock State Park from Redmond, travel 5 miles north on U.S. Highway 97 to the small town of Terrebonne. At the flashing yellow light, turn right onto B Avenue (this turns into Smith Rock Way after the first stop sign). Travel 3.3 miles northeast, following the signs to Smith Rock State Park. To continue to the trailhead, head back out of Smith Rock State Park to Smith Rock Way. Turn left onto Smith Rock Way and continue about 4.3 miles to Lone Pine Road. Turn left onto Lone Pine Road and go about 4.4 miles to Forest Service Road 5710. Turn left onto Forest Service Road 5710 (you'll pass Skull Hollow Campground on your left). Follow Forest Service Road 5710 as it winds up Skull Hollow Canyon for 2.6 miles. Turn left onto Forest Service Road 57.

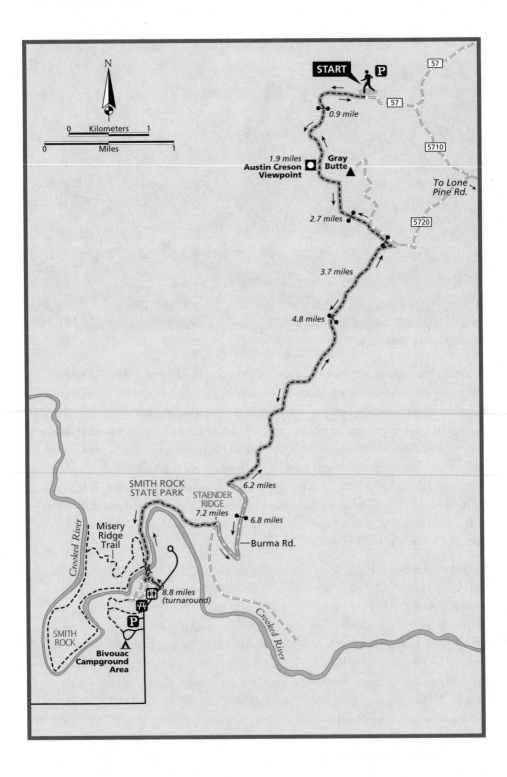

START

P

57

0.9 mile

57

5710

1.9 miles
Austin Creson
Viewpoint

Gray
Butte

To Lone
Pine Rd.

2.7 miles

5720

3.7 miles

4.8 miles

6.2 miles

SMITH ROCK
STATE PARK

STAENDER
RIDGE

7.2 miles

6.8 miles

Burma Rd.

Misery
Ridge
Trail

8.8 miles
(turnaround)

SMITH
ROCK

Crooked River

Crooked River

Bivouac
Campground
Area

N

Kilometers

0   1

Miles

0   1

Proceed 0.6 mile to a gravel parking area and the Gray Butte Trailhead on the left side of the road. *DeLorme: Oregon Atlas & Gazetteer:* Page 51 A8.

TRAIL DIRT

0.0 The singletrack trail starts on the northeast edge of Gray Butte. The trail climbs slowly as it rounds the north edge of the butte.

0.9 Go through a green metal gate and continue your fun cruise through this magnificent high-desert landscape. (To the west you'll have awesome views of the Three Sisters Mountains, Broken Top, Black Butte, and Mount Jefferson.)

1.9 (**Sidetrip:** You may want to check out the side trail on your right, which leads to the Austin Creson viewpoint. A memorial plaque for Austin Creson is located at this point and is dedicated to his hard work on planning the Gray Butte Trail. From this vantage point you'll have more breathtaking views of the Central Oregon Cascades. Continue your fun trek as the trail swings around the west side of Gray Butte.)

2.7 Go through a green metal gate.

3.6 Turn right at the trail fork. Continue your spectacular journey on this singletrack trail as it sweeps across ridges and offers grand views to the west of the Central Cascades.

3.7 Cross a dirt road and continue running on the signed Gray Butte Trail.

4.8 Go through a green metal gate.

5.2 Cross a gravel road and continue straight on the singletrack trail as it ascends a hill. After 200 yards you'll arrive at a trail fork. Turn left and continue your trek on the signed singletrack trail.

5.4 Cross a dirt road and continue straight on the singletrack Gray Butte Trail.

6.2 Arrive at the junction with Burma Road. Go left onto Burma Road and head downhill on the steep doubletrack road. (Enjoy the spectacular views of the Crooked River Canyon from this high vantage point atop Staender Ridge. You are now within the boundaries of Smith Rock State Park. If you are not planning on doing a car shuttle, this is an optional turnaround point. If you have your trailhound with you, be sure to put his leash on while in the park boundaries or face a stiff fine.)

7.2 Arrive next to a large tunnel and irrigation canal. Turn right on an unsigned singletrack trail that zigzags steeply to the canyon floor. Ignore any side trails that go off the main trail as you descend.

7.4 Arrive at the canyon floor and turn right onto a singletrack trail. Glide along the smooth singletrack trail as it parallels the Crooked River through a magnificent canyon framed by towering rock spires.

8.4 Turn left and cross a wooden footbridge over the Crooked River. After you cross you'll join up with a doubletrack road that heads uphill. Turn left on the steeper singletrack trail that winds steeply uphill.

8.8 Arrive at the Smith Rock State Park main parking lot and picnic area for the park at the top of the rim. This is your ending point if you are doing the car shuttle. (**Option:** If you are feeling tough and want to complete an out-and-back journey, retrace the same route back to your starting point at 17.6 miles.)

TRAIL FOOD

La Siesta, 8320 North Highway 97, Terrebonne, OR 97760, (541) 548–4848

Seventh Street Brew House, 855 Southwest 7th Street, Redmond, OR 97756, (541) 923–1795

45: Carroll Rim–Painted Hills Overlook

Region/area:	Prineville
Pain:	3
Gain:	3
Distance:	2.7 miles
Elevation gain:	600 feet
Time:	45 minutes to 1 hour
The route:	A nice singletrack trail that climbs to the top of Carroll Rim, providing a commanding view of the spectacular painted hills located in the John Day Fossil Beds National Monument. The route then heads up the Painted Hills Overlook Trail and provides another look at the spectacular colors of these unique hills.
Trail surface:	100% smooth dirt
Sun exposure:	100%
Runability:	100%
Season:	Year-round
Other users:	Hikers
Canine compatibility:	Leashed dogs permitted
Permits/fees:	None
Trail contact:	John Day Fossil Beds National Monument, Kimberly, OR, (541) 987–2333, www.nps.gov/joda
Map:	USGS Painted Hills (7.5' series)

Trail scoop: This route takes you on a journey to the multicolored hills in the John Day Fossil Beds National Monument. You'll start by running to the top of Carroll

The spectacular Painted Hills in the John Day Fossil Beds National Monument

Rim, where you'll have a wonderful view of Sutton Mountain and the surrounding colorful claystone hills. After a fun descent you'll head up the Painted Hills Overlook Trail, where you'll be able to see the rounded hills from a different perspective. If you seek solitude this remote trail run is for you. This trail is a scorcher in the summer—be sure to bring water with you because no water (or rest rooms) are available at the trailhead.

Finding the trailhead: From Prineville travel 45.2 miles east on U.S. Highway 26 to the junction with Burnt Ranch Road, where a sign indicates JOHN DAY FOSSIL BEDS NATIONAL MONUMENT–PAINTED HILLS UNIT. Turn left (north) and go 5.7 miles. Turn left onto Bear Creek Road and proceed 0.9 mile to the turnoff for the Carroll Rim Trailhead. Turn left and then take an immediate right into the gravel parking area on the right. *DeLorme: Oregon Atlas & Gazetteer:* Page 80 B3.

TRAIL DIRT

0.0 From the parking area go left on a gravel road, cross Bear Creek Road, and begin running uphill on the signed Carroll Rim Trail. As you climb enjoy the commanding view of the surrounding painted hills.

0.7 Arrive at the top of Carroll Rim. Catch your breath before you zoom downhill on the same trail.

1.5 Cross Bear Creek Road and jog up the gravel road past your car to the start of the Painted Hills Overlook Trail.

1.6 Start running on the Painted Hills Overlook Trail. Pass interpretive signs on

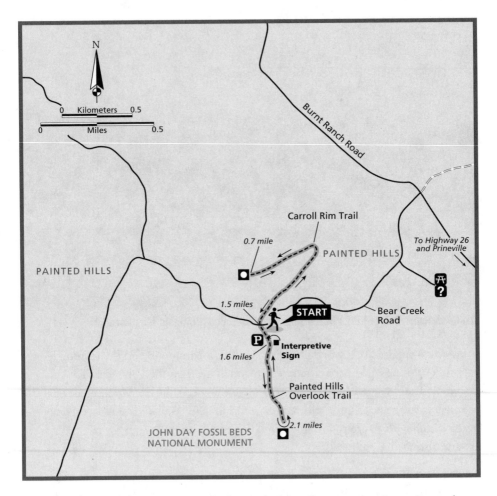

your left and power up the wide dirt path that takes you to a viewpoint at the top of the hill.

2.1 Arrive at a viewpoint. Enjoy the intense red, gold, and yellow colors of the painted hills before you head downhill on the same route back to your starting point.

2.7 Arrive at the trailhead.

A Rainbow of Colors

The round multicolored hills in this national monument are made of claystone. Thirty million years ago layers of ash were deposited in this area from volcanoes erupting to the west. Over millions of years the forces of nature have carved and shaped the hills you see today. Different elements such as aluminum, silicon, iron, magnesium, manganese, sodium, calcium, titanium, and others have combined to produce minerals that have unique properties and colors. The colors of the hills change with the weather. When it rains the clay absorbs water, causing more light reflection and changing the color of the hills from red to pink and from light brown to yellow-gold. As the hills dry out, the soil contracts, causing surface cracking that diffuses the light and makes the color of the hills deepen. Plants can't grow on the painted hills because the clay is so dense that moisture can't penetrate the surface.

TRAIL FOOD

Ranchero Mexican Restaurant, 969 Northwest 3rd Street, Prineville, OR 97754, (541) 416–0103

46: Steins Pillar

Region/area:	Prineville
Pain:	2
Gain:	2
Distance:	5.2 miles out and back
Elevation gain:	350 feet
Time:	1 to 1.25 hours
The route:	This singletrack route takes you on a trek through a forest and sagebrush landscape to dramatic 350-foot Steins Pillar. Stairs. Views.
Trail surface:	98% smooth dirt, 2% rocky
Sun exposure:	60%
Runability:	100%
Season:	May through October
Other users:	Hikers, mountain bikers, equestrians
Canine compatibility:	Dogs permitted
Permits/fees:	None
Trail contact:	Ochoco National Forest, Prineville, OR, (541) 416–6500, www.fs.fed.us/r6/centraloregon
Map:	USGS Salt Butte and Steins Pillar (7.5' series)

Trail scoop: Those seeking solitude will enjoy this singletrack route that ascends a

Steins Pillar

ridge through a ponderosa pine forest and sagebrush landscape and then heads downhill to a stunning viewpoint of 350-foot Steins Pillar. No rest rooms or water are available at the trailhead.

Finding the trailhead: Head 9.1 miles east of Prineville on U.S. Highway 26. Turn left (north) onto Mill Creek Road (Forest Service Road 33). Travel 6.7 miles on Mill Creek Road (the road turns to gravel after 5.2 miles) to the junction with Forest Service Road 500. Turn right onto Forest Service Road 500 and continue 2.1 miles to the trailhead on the left side of the road. *DeLorme: Oregon Atlas & Gazetteer:* Page 80 C2.

TRAIL DIRT

0.0 Start on the dirt track next to a Steins Pillar trail sign.

0.3 Begin climbing a ridge through Douglas fir and ponderosa pine forest.

1.2 The trail starts descending.

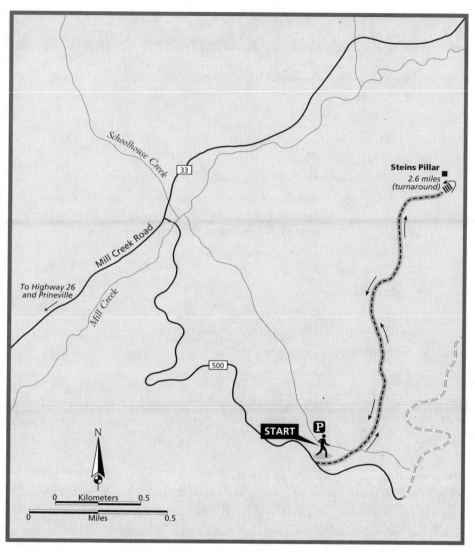

2.3 Reach a viewpoint of Steins Pillar on your left.

2.4 Descend on a long series of wood steps.

2.6 Arrive at the base of 350-foot Steins Pillar (your turnaround point). From here, retrace the route back to the trailhead.

5.2 Arrive at the trailhead.

TRAIL FOOD

Apple Peddler Restaurant, 1485 Northeast 3rd Street, Prineville, OR 97754, (541) 416–8949

47: Eagle Rock Loop

Region/area:	Sisters
Pain:	1
Gain:	4
Distance:	5.6-mile loop
Elevation gain:	150 feet
Time:	45 minutes to 1 hour
The route:	A fun singletrack and doubletrack route that winds through a ponderosa and lodgepole pine forest at the edge of Sisters city limits. Bridge crossings.
Trail surface:	85% smooth dirt, 15% rocky
Sun exposure:	40%
Runability:	100%
Season:	Year-round (snow can be present in the winter months)
Other users:	Mountain bikers, hikers
Canine compatibility:	Dogs permitted
Permits/fees:	None
Trail contact:	Deschutes National Forest, Sisters Ranger District, Sisters, OR, (541) 549–7700, www.fs.fed.us/r6/centraloregon
Map:	USGS Sisters and Three Creek Butte (7.5' series)

Trail scoop: This is a fast and sporty sprint located right on the edge of the Sisters city limits. It takes you through a sunny, open lodgepole and ponderosa pine forest, saunters along bubbling Squaw Creek, and then loops back to your starting point. Tread carefully through the rounded river stone found in some drainages. No rest rooms or water are available at the trailhead.

Finding the trailhead: From downtown Sisters, head west on Highway 20. Just at the edge of the city limits, turn left (south) onto Elm Street. Travel 0.5 mile and turn left onto Tyee Drive and park on the right side of the road. Immediately on the right is a trail sign that marks the start of this route. *DeLorme: Oregon Atlas & Gazetteer:* Page 50 B4.

TRAIL DIRT

0.0 Start running on the singletrack trail that begins at the Sisters Mountain Bike Trailhead sign.

On the Eagle Rock Loop Trail

0.3 Cross a doubletrack road and continue running on the singletrack trail as it twists and turns through an open sunny forest. As you are cruising on this trail, be on the lookout for the brown mountain bike trail markers.

1.6 Cross a wood bridge over a small irrigation canal. After you cross the bridge, cross a doubletrack dirt road and continue running on the singletrack trail.

1.9 Cross a large gravel road and continue on the doubletrack trail.

2.2 Turn left onto a signed doubletrack road.

2.3 Turn right onto a singletrack trail and then take another immediate right at the trail sign that indicates EAGLE ROCK LOOP. (If you end up crossing a bridge over an irrigation canal, you have missed this last turn. At this point the trail parallels the Squaw Creek irrigation canal and travels through an old burn area.)

2.9 Turn left onto a grassy doubletrack road.

3.0 Turn left onto another doubletrack road.

3.1 Turn right onto another doubletrack road.

4.0 Cross a gravel road and continue straight on the doubletrack trail. About 100 yards past this intersection, turn left on a singletrack trail and cross a bridge over a small irrigation canal where a sign reads SISTERS 2 MILES. You'll rejoin this fast singletrack for 1.6 miles as it whips through the forest back to your starting point.

5.6 Arrive at the trailhead.

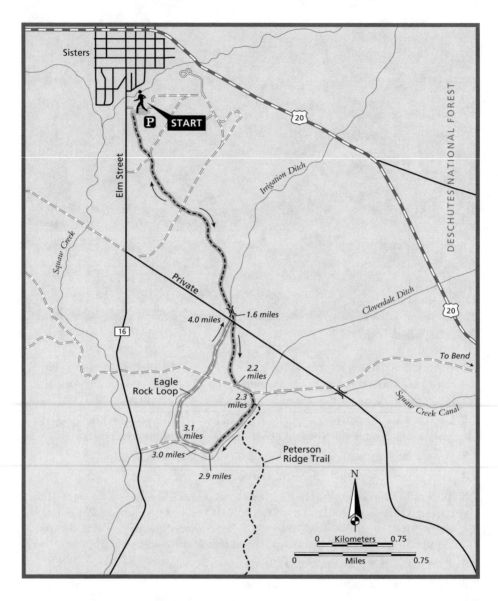

TRAIL FOOD

El Rancho Grande, 150 East Cascade Avenue, Sisters, OR 97759, (541) 549–3594
Papandrea's Pizzeria, 442 East Hood Avenue, Sisters, OR 97759, (541) 549–6081
Sisters Bakery, 251 East Cascade Avenue, Sisters, OR 97759, (541) 549–0361
Sisters Coffee Company, 273 West Hood Street, Sisters, OR 97759, (800)
    524–JAVA, www.sisterscoffee.com

48: Black Butte

Region/area:	Sisters
Pain:	4
Gain:	4
Distance:	3.8 miles out and back
Elevation gain:	1,585 feet
Time:	1.25 to 2 hours
The route:	A nice dirt path leading to the spectacular summit of Black Butte in the Deschutes National Forest. Mountain views.
Trail surface:	90% smooth dirt, 10% rocky
Sun exposure:	90%
Runability:	100%
Season:	June through October
Other users:	Hikers
Canine compatibility:	Dogs permitted
Permits/fees:	$5.00 Northwest Forest Pass, purchased by calling (800) 270–7504, or online at www.naturenw.org.
Trail contact:	Deschutes National Forest, Sisters Ranger District, Sisters, OR, (541) 549–7700, www.fs.fed.us/r6/centraloregon
Map:	USGS Black Butte and Little Squaw Back (7.5' series)

Trail scoop: This tough route takes you to the top of one of the tallest cinder cones in the state. The strenuous climb to the 6,436-foot summit can be hot and dusty, but the close-up views of the Cascade Mountains well make up for it. Once you reach the top, be sure to check out the historic fire lookouts. Consider bringing an extra layer for the sometimes-chilly summit. No rest rooms or water are available at the trailhead.

Finding the trailhead: Head 6 miles west of Sisters on Highway 20 and turn right onto Green Ridge Road (Forest Service Road 11). Go 3.8 miles to Forest Service Road 1110. Turn left onto Forest Service Road 1110 and travel 4.2 miles to a road junction. Turn right and continue 1.1 miles to a large parking area and the trailhead. *DeLorme: Oregon Atlas & Gazetteer:* Page 50 A4.

TRAIL DIRT

0.0 Start running on the well-traveled singletrack trail up a moderate grade through stands of grand fir, white bark pine, and shimmering aspen trees.

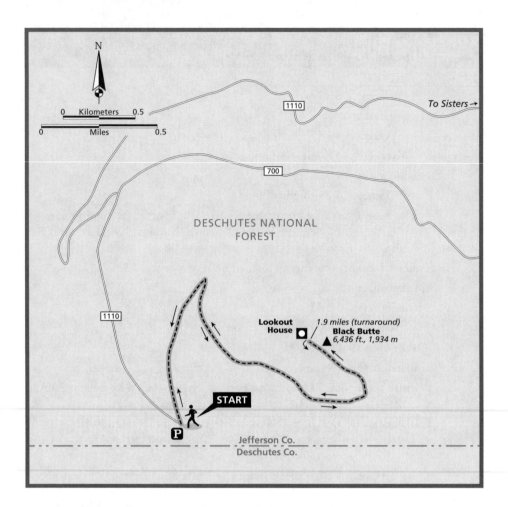

1.7 Veer right and continue your push for the summit.

1.9 Arrive at the spectacular 6,436-foot summit. Enjoy the awesome mountain views while you catch your breath and then blast downhill on the same route back to your starting point.

3.8 Arrive at the trailhead.

TRAIL FOOD

El Rancho Grande, 150 East Cascade Avenue, Sisters, OR 97759, (541) 549–3594

Papandrea's Pizzeria, 442 East Hood Avenue, Sisters, OR 97759, (541) 549–6081

Sisters Bakery, 251 East Cascade Avenue, Sisters, OR 97759, (541) 549–0361

Sisters Coffee Company, 273 West Hood Street, Sisters, OR 97759, (800) 524–JAVA, www.sisterscoffee.com

Quite a lineup...
Oregon's Cascade Mountains from north to south:
Mount Hood (11,239 feet)
Mount Jefferson (10,497 feet)
Three Fingered Jack (7,841 feet)
Mount Washington (7,749 feet)
Black Butte (6,436 feet)
North Sister (10,094 feet)
Middle Sister (10,054 feet)
South Sister (10,385 feet)
Broken Top (9,175 feet)
Mount Bachelor (9,065 feet)

49: West Metolius River

Region/area:	Sisters
Pain:	2
Gain:	5
Distance:	5 miles out and back (with longer options)
Elevation gain:	200 feet
Time:	45 minutes to 1.5 hours
The route:	An exquisite river run through a sunny ponderosa pine forest to Wizard Falls Fish Hatchery.
Trail surface:	65% smooth dirt, 35% rocky
Sun exposure:	10%
Runability:	100%
Season:	April through November
Other users:	Hikers
Canine compatibility:	Dogs permitted
Permits/fees:	None
Trail contact:	Deschutes National Forest, Sisters Ranger District, Sisters, OR, (541) 549–7700, www.fs.fed.us/r6/centraloregon
Maps:	Imus Geographics: Metolius River–Black Butte–Green Ridge; Green Trails Whitewater River; USGS Black Butte, Candle Creek, and Prairie Farm Spring (7.5' series)

The spring-fed Metolius River

Trail scoop: This spectacular riverside trail will make your spirit soar. The crystal-clear waters of the wild and scenic Metolius River are center stage and the parklike ponderosa pine forest, lush streamside vegetation, and sweet singletrack make up the award-winning cast. For the encore you can explore the Wizard Falls Fish Hatchery, with its viewing ponds, interpretive displays, and a shady picnic area. Rest rooms are available in the campground (no water).

Finding the trailhead: From Sisters head 10 miles west on U.S. Highway 20 to Camp Sherman Road (Forest Service Road 14). Turn right (north) and travel 2.7 miles to the junction with Forest Service Road 1419. Turn left and go 2.3 miles to another road junction and stop sign. Continue straight (you're now on Forest Service Road 1420) for another 3.4 miles to the junction with Forest Service Road 400. Turn right onto Forest Service Road 400 toward Lower Canyon Creek Campground and go 0.9 mile through the campground to the road's end and trailhead. *DeLorme: Oregon Atlas & Gazetteer:* Page 50 A3.

TRAIL DIRT

0.0 Start this stunning river run at the wood trail sign for West Metolius River located in the Lower Canyon Creek Campground. A sign indicates you'll reach Wizard Falls in 2.5 miles. (The trail dips in and out, following the river's contours through a sunny ponderosa pine forest. Watch your footwork as you travel through some rocky areas next to the river's edge.)

0.3 (Look off to your right to view an amazing natural spring that splashes into the river from underground. As you cruise on this sweet singletrack trail you'll enjoy

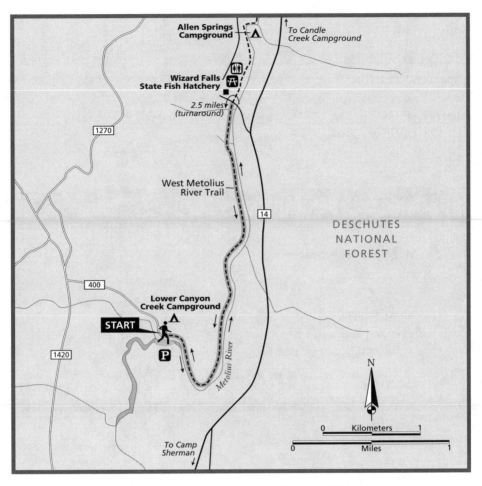

Mother Nature's air-conditioning as the wind whips off the river, creating a cooling breeze. You'll sail past lush riverside vegetation and be mesmerized by the soothing sounds of the river.)

2.5 Arrive at Wizard Falls Fish Hatchery. (If you are feeling curious, take the time to explore the fish hatchery before you head back to the trailhead. Water and rest rooms are available at the hatchery.) (**Option:** If you want to tackle a longer river route, continue on the trail on the west or east side of the river for about 5 more miles.)

The Origin of the Metolius River

The Metolius River originates as a natural spring at the base of Black Butte before winding its way north through the Metolius Basin into Lake Billy Chinook. Numerous springs, fed via porous volcanic rock high in the Central Cascade Mountains, continue to feed the river along its entire length, keeping the flow rate fairly steady at 1,200 to 1,800 cubic feet per second.

TRAIL FOOD

El Rancho Grande, 150 East Cascade Avenue, Sisters, OR 97759, (541) 549–3594
Papandrea's Pizzeria, 442 East Hood Avenue, Sisters, OR 97759, (541) 549–6081
Sisters Bakery, 251 East Cascade Avenue, Sisters, OR 97759, (541) 549–0361
Sisters Coffee Company, 273 West Hood Street, Sisters, OR 97759, (800)
    524–JAVA, www.sisterscoffee.com

50: Canyon Creek Meadows Loop

Region/area:	Sisters
Pain:	2
Gain:	4
Distance:	5.5-mile loop
Elevation gain:	675 feet
Time:	1 to 1.25 hours
The route:	This route travels past Jack Lake and takes you to a spectacular high-alpine wildflower meadow at the base of the craggy spires of Three Fingered Jack. Mountain and lake views. Bridge crossings.
Trail surface:	100% smooth dirt
Sun exposure:	70%
Runability:	100%
Season:	June through October
Other users:	Hikers
Canine compatibility:	Leashed dogs permitted
Permits/fees:	$5.00 Northwest Forest Pass, purchased by calling (800) 270–7504, or online at www.naturenw.org. Free self-issue wilderness permits are required and are available at the trailhead.
Trail contact:	Deschutes National Forest, Sisters Ranger District, Sisters, OR, (541) 549–7700, www.fs.fed.us/r6/centraloregon
Maps:	USGS Three Fingered Jack and Marion Lake (7.5' series); Geo-Graphics Mount Jefferson Wilderness

Trail scoop: High mountain scenery is the spotlight of this popular trail. The route takes you past Jack Lake and then enters spectacular Canyon Creek Meadows. This

View of Three Fingered Jack

high-alpine meadow has a profusion of bright purple lupine and brilliant red Indian paintbrush blooms in the summer months. You'll also enjoy a stunning view of the craggy spires of 7,841-foot Three Fingered Jack. Rest rooms (no water) are available at the trailhead.

Finding the trailhead: From Sisters head west on U.S. Highway 20 for 12 miles to Jack Lake Road (Forest Service Road 12). Turn right and travel 4.3 miles on Jack Lake Road to the junction with Forest Service Road 1230. Turn left onto Forest Service Road 1230 and go 1.7 miles. Turn left onto Forest Service Road 1234 (the road turns to gravel here) and travel about 6.2 more miles to Jack Lake and the trailhead. *DeLorme: Oregon Atlas & Gazetteer:* Page 50 A2.

TRAIL DIRT

0.0 Start running on the smooth singletrack trail signed CANYON CREEK MEADOWS. (This fast trail sails past quiet Jack Lake.)

0.2 Turn left toward Canyon Creek. (The trail leads you into an amazing high-alpine meadow filled with bubbling creeks and colorful wildflowers.)

1.7 Turn left at the trail fork.

2.0 Arrive at a high-alpine meadow with a stunning view of 7,841-foot Three Fingered Jack. After admiring the view turn around and head back on the same trail.

2.3 Turn left at the trail junction.

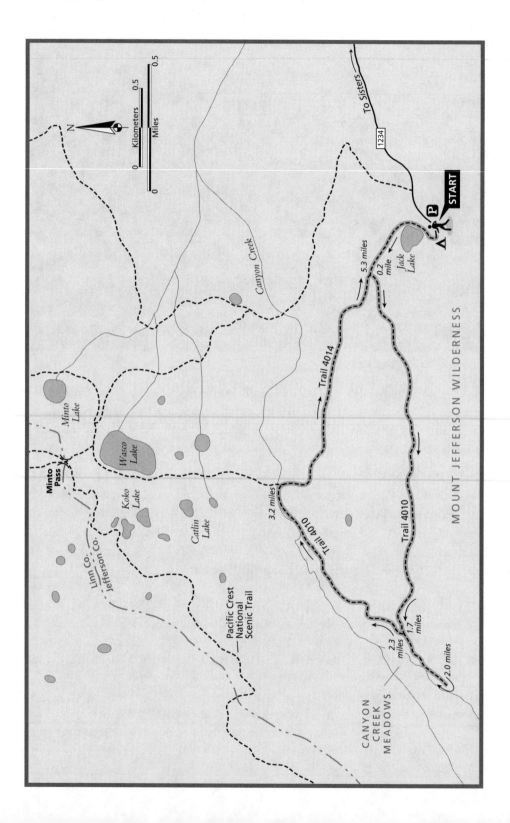

N

Kilometers
0   0.5

Miles
0   0.5

To Sisters

1234

START

P

△

Jack Lake

0.2 mile

5.3 miles

Trail 4014

Canyon Creek

Minto Lake

Wasco Lake

Koko Lake

Catlin Lake

Minto Pass

Linn Co.
Jefferson Co.

Pacific Crest National Scenic Trail

3.2 miles

Trail 4010

Trail 4010

2.3 miles

1.7 miles

2.0 miles

CANYON CREEK MEADOWS

MOUNT JEFFERSON WILDERNESS

3.2 Turn right at the trail junction.

5.3 Continue straight (left) toward Jack Lake and the trailhead.

5.5 Arrive at the trailhead.

TRAIL FOOD

El Rancho Grande, 150 East Cascade Avenue, Sisters, OR 97759, (541) 549–3594

Papandrea's Pizzeria, 442 East Hood Avenue, Sisters, OR 97759, (541) 549–6081

Sisters Bakery, 251 East Cascade Avenue, Sisters, OR 97759, (541) 549–0361

Sisters Coffee Company, 273 West Hood Street, Sisters, OR 97759, (800)
524–JAVA, www.sisterscoffee.com

51: Suttle Lake Loop

Region/area:	Sisters
Pain:	1
Gain:	3
Distance:	3.6-mile loop
Elevation gain:	5 feet
Time:	30 minutes to 1 hour
The route:	Wide dirt path that follows the shoreline of Suttle Lake in the Deschutes National Forest. Mountain views. Bridge crossings.
Trail surface:	96% smooth dirt, 2% rocky, 2% paved
Sun exposure:	25%
Runability:	100%
Season:	May through November
Other users:	Hikers, mountain bikers
Canine compatibility:	Leashed dogs permitted
Permits/fees:	None
Trail contact:	Deschutes National Forest, Sisters Ranger District, Sisters, OR, (541) 549–7700, www.fs.fed.us/r6/centraloregon
Map:	USGS Black Butte (7.5' series)

Trail scoop: Do you love lake runs? If so you'll get in the groove when you run on the smooth singletrack that circles Suttle Lake. The rhythm is fast and the view of the

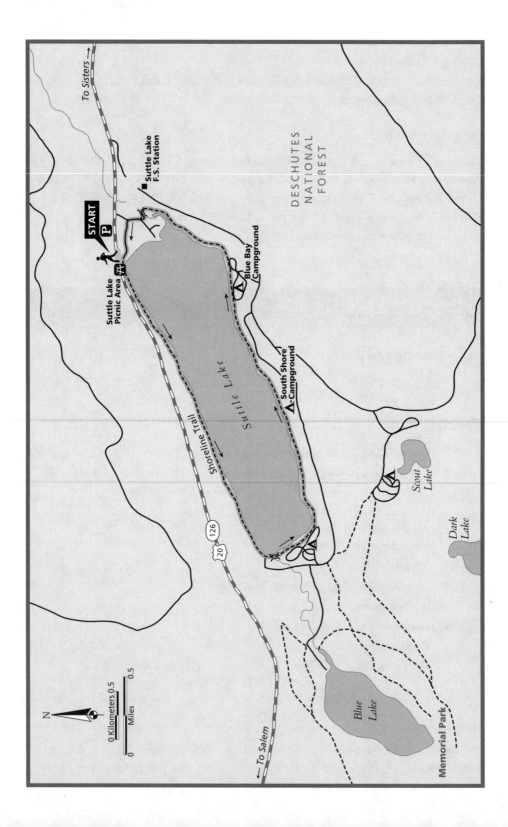

Checking out the singletrack action at Suttle Lake

snow-covered crest of 7,749-foot Mount Washington is phenomenal. Be sure to cool off in the lake after your run. No rest rooms or water are available at the trailhead.

Finding the trailhead: From Sisters head 12.5 miles west on Highway 20. Turn left at the Suttle Lake–Marina & Resort sign onto the Suttle Lake entrance road. Proceed on the entrance road and take the first right turn signed for Cinder Beach. Go 0.3 mile to a parking lot next to the lake and the trailhead. *DeLorme: Oregon Atlas & Gazetteer:* Page 50 A3.

TRAIL DIRT

0.0 From the picnic area at Cinder Beach, start running around the lake in a counterclockwise direction on the signed Shoreline Trail.

1.4 Continue straight across a paved road at a boat ramp and then cross an arched wood bridge over an outlet creek. After you cross the bridge, follow the trail as it hugs the shoreline of the lake. On a clear day look for the pointy summit of Mount Washington above the tree line.

1.6 Cross a paved road and pick up the trail on the other side; surf on the smooth singletrack as it hugs the lakeshore.

2.5 Cross another paved road and pick up the trail on the other side, which takes you through a shady picnic area.

2.9 Cross another paved road and continue grooving on the dirt path on the other side.

3.4 Arrive at a trail fork. Veer left at the Suttle Tie Trailhead sign and then run across a wood bridge over Link Creek. After you run across the bridge, take a very sharp right turn and watch for the brown trail signs.

3.5 Start running on a paved road and follow the brown trail signs marking the route.

3.6 Arrive at the Cinder Beach parking area and your starting point.

TRAIL FOOD

El Rancho Grande, 150 East Cascade Avenue, Sisters, OR 97759, (541) 549–3594

Papandrea's Pizzeria, 442 East Hood Avenue, Sisters, OR 97759, (541) 549–6081

Sisters Bakery, 251 East Cascade Avenue, Sisters, OR 97759, (541) 549–0361

Sisters Coffee Company, 273 West Hood Street, Sisters, OR 97759, (800) 524–JAVA, www.sisterscoffee.com

52: Tam McArthur Rim

Region/area:	Sisters
Pain:	4
Gain:	5
Distance:	5 miles out and back
Elevation gain:	1,200 feet
Time:	1.5 minutes to 2.5 hours
The route:	This singletrack route begins at Three Creeks Lake and winds to the top of spectacular Tam McArthur Rim. Mountain views.
Trail surface:	70% smooth dirt, 30% rocky
Sun exposure:	65%
Runability:	100%
Season:	Mid-June through October
Other users:	Hikers
Canine compatibility:	Dogs permitted
Permits/fees:	$5.00 Northwest Forest Pass, purchased by calling (800) 270–7504, or online at www.naturenw.org.
Trail contact:	Deschutes National Forest, Sisters Ranger District, Sisters, OR, (541) 549–7700, www.fs.fed.us/r6/centraloregon
Maps:	USGS Broken Top (7.5' series); Geo-Graphics Three Sisters Wilderness

Running along the ridgeline of the Tam McArthur Rim Trail

Trail scoop: This route takes you to the top of Tam McArthur Rim—a vast windswept ridge in the Three Sisters Wilderness. Twisted white bark pine, delicate high-alpine wildflowers, and endless mountain views are your reward after your steep climb to the spectacular rim viewpoint. No rest rooms or water are available at the trailhead.

Finding the trailhead: From U.S. Highway 20 in Sisters, turn south onto Elm Street (Forest Service Road 16). Head 15.6 miles (the road turns to gravel after 14 miles) to the trailhead parking area located on the left side of the road at Three Creeks Lake. *DeLorme: Oregon Atlas & Gazetteer:* Page 50 C4.

TRAIL DIRT

0.0 Start running a steep uphill at the wood trailhead sign for Tam McArthur Rim #4078. The sign indicates it is 2.5 miles to the summit viewpoint. (This trail climbs brutally the first 0.8 mile through a high-alpine forest. Open meadows, old tree logs, and bright purple lupine line the trail. The trail leads you to the top of the wide-open windswept ridge where white bark pine thrive. Follow the trail west along the dramatic ridgeline. Along the way spur trails will head off the trail. Continue on the main trail, ignoring these spur trails.)

2.3 Turn right at an unmarked trail intersection.

2.5 Arrive at a spectacular viewpoint from a lofty rocky escarpment overlooking Three Creeks Lake. (From this gorgeous vantage point, you'll have views of the Three Creeks Lake Basin to the east, Broken Top and the Three Sisters Mountains to the west, Mount Washington and Mount Jefferson to the north-

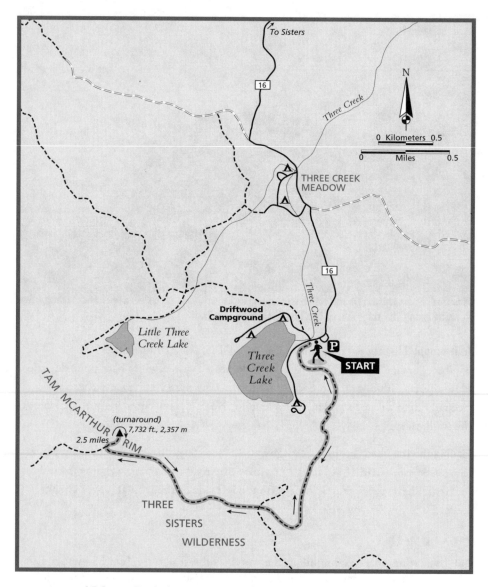

west, and Mount Bachelor to the south.) After enjoying the mesmerizing view head back on the same route to your starting point.

5.0 Arrive at the trailhead.

TRAIL FOOD

El Rancho Grande, 150 East Cascade Avenue, Sisters, OR 97759, (541) 549–3594

Papandrea's Pizzeria, 442 East Hood Avenue, Sisters, OR 97759, (541) 549–6081

Sisters Bakery, 251 East Cascade Avenue, Sisters, OR 97759, (541) 549–0361

Sisters Coffee Company, 273 West Hood Street, Sisters, OR 97759, (800) 524–JAVA, www.sisterscoffee.com

Region/area:	Sisters
Pain:	3
Gain:	4
Distance:	7.2 miles out and back
Elevation gain:	700 feet
Time:	1.50 hours to 2 hours
The route:	Singletrack trail that weaves through a cool forest to a high-alpine meadow in the Three Sisters Wilderness. Mountain views. Bridge crossings.
Trail surface:	90% smooth dirt, 10% rocky
Sun exposure:	40%
Runability:	100%
Season:	Mid-July through October
Other users:	Hikers, equestrians
Canine compatibility:	Leashed dogs permitted
Permits/fees:	A free wilderness permit is required. The self-issue permit can be obtained at the permit station, located on the trail 0.9 mile from the trailhead.
Trail contact:	Deschutes National Forest, Sisters Ranger District, Sisters, OR, (541) 549–7700, www.fs.fed.us/r6/centraloregon
Maps:	USGS Broken Top (7.5' series); Geo-Graphics Three Sisters Wilderness

Trail scoop: This brisk forest run winds through the heart of the Three Sisters Wilderness, where you'll dash over creeks and arrive at a gorgeous high-alpine meadow with awesome views of Broken Top and South Sister. As you are loping along the trail, be on the lookout for horse pies that are fairly common on this popular equestrian trail. Be sure to wear mosquito repellent if you are running this trail in early summer. Also, bring water with you—this trail can be very hot and dusty and no water is available at the trailhead.

Finding the trailhead: From Highway 20 in Sisters, turn south onto Elm Street (this street turns into Forest Service Road 16) and travel 14 miles to the Park Meadow Trailhead on the right side of the road. Turn right at the trailhead sign onto a rough gravel road. *(If you are driving a passenger car, you'll need to heed caution when driving on this rocky, rutted road.)* If you are in a passenger car, you can travel for 1 mile on

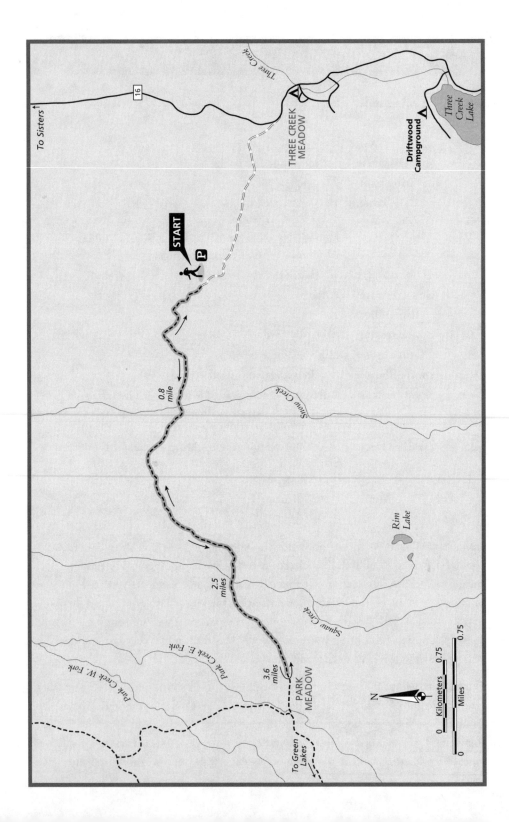

To Sisters

16

Three Creek

THREE CREEK
MEADOW

Driftwood
Campground

Three
Creek
Lake

START

P

0.8
mile

Snow Creek

2.5
miles

Rim
Lake

Squaw Creek

3.6
miles

PARK
MEADOW

Park Creek E. Fork

Park Creek W. Fork

To Green
Lakes

N

0   Kilometers   0.75

0   Miles   0.75

this dirt road and park beside the road. You can then walk the remaining 0.1 mile to the trailhead. If you have a high clearance vehicle, you can drive 1.1 miles to the trailhead. *DeLorme: Oregon Atlas & Gazetteer:* Page 50 C4.

TRAIL DIRT:

0.0 Start running at the trailhead sign that reads PARK MEADOW 3.75/ GREEN LAKES TRAIL 6.75. This fun forest trek weaves in and out of a hemlock, cedar, and blue spruce forest.

0.8 Cross a shallow stream and arrive at a four-way junction. Continue straight toward Park Meadow. Be sure to pick up a free self-issue wilderness permit at the permit station at this junction.

On the Park Meadow Trail

1.2 Cross a log bridge over a bubbling creek. Continue running on the forested trail that has periodic rocky sections. (After running for about 2 miles, you'll get sneak peeks of Broken Top and South Sister above the tree line.)

2.5 Cross a log bridge over Squaw Creek.

3.4 Arrive at the Park Meadow. (You'll have unsurpassed views of Broken Top and South Sister from the gorgeous wildflower-filled meadow.) To continue across the meadow, cross a log bridge over a fast-flowing creek and continue on the trail across the meadow for about another 0.2 mile.

3.6 Arrive at the route's turnaround point. Be sure to bask in the sun and enjoy the spectacular mountain views before retracing your route to your starting point.

7.2 Arrive at the trailhead.

TRAIL FOOD

El Rancho Grande, 150 East Cascade Avenue, Sisters, OR 97759, (541) 549–3594

Papandrea's Pizzeria, 442 East Hood Avenue, Sisters, OR 97759, (541) 549–6081

Sisters Bakery, 251 East Cascade Avenue, Sisters, OR 97759, (541) 549–0361

Sisters Coffee Company, 273 West Hood Street, Sisters, OR 97759, (800) 524–JAVA, www.sisterscoffee.com

54: First Street Rapids

Region/area:	Bend
Pain:	1
Gain:	2
Distance:	6 miles out and back
Elevation gain:	120 feet
Time:	50 minutes to 1.25 hours
The route:	This easy wood-chip trail begins at First Street Rapids Park and follows the Deschutes River north through a scenic river canyon filled with ponderosa pine and juniper trees, a golf course, and residential houses. Mountain views.
Trail surface:	98% wood chip, 2% paved
Sun exposure:	95%
Runability:	100%
Season:	Year-round
Other users:	Hikers, mountain bikers
Canine compatibility:	Leashed dogs permitted
Permits/fees:	None
Trail contact:	Bend Metro Park & Recreation District, Bend, OR, (541) 389-7275, www.bendparksandrec.org
Map:	USGS Bend (7.5' series)

Trail scoop: This popular wood-chip trail takes you along a scenic section of the rambling Deschutes River. The trail begins at First Street Rapids Park and heads north along the river's edge. After about a mile you'll parallel a golf course as the trail winds through a mix of juniper, sage, and yellow-barked ponderosa pine trees. The last half of the trail winds high on the canyon rim and affords stunning views of Mount Washington and Black Butte to the northwest and the Deschutes River far below. Rest rooms are available at the trailhead (no water).

Finding the trailhead: From U.S. Highway 97 in Bend, turn right onto Division Street. Go 0.8 mile and turn right onto Revere Avenue. Continue 0.2 mile and turn left onto Hill Street. Proceed 0.2 mile and turn right onto Portland Avenue. Go 0.2 mile and turn right onto First Street. Continue 0.3 mile to where the street dead-ends at First Street Rapids Park. DeLorme: *Oregon Atlas & Gazetteer:* Page 51 D6.

The Deschutes River Canyon in Bend

TRAIL DIRT

0.0 From First Street Rapids Park, begin running north on the wood-chip trail that parallels the scenic Deschutes River.

0.7 Turn left on the wood-chip trail (don't go right toward the golf course). The trail intersects with the paved Mount Washington Drive. Turn right and follow the wood-chip trail downhill as it parallels Mount Washington Drive. (Look for the small Deschutes River Trail signs marking the trail.)

0.8 Turn left and cross Mount Washington Drive. Pick up the wood-chip trail on the other side. (The trail parallels a paved trail for a short distance but then turns back to wood chip only. The trail continues to parallel the golf course and then enters a forest corridor that passes through several residential areas.)

2.0 Cross Archie Briggs Road and continue running on the wood-chip trail on the other side.

2.3 The trail crosses Northcliff Street in a residential area and then hugs the ridge-line high above the Deschutes River. (From this section of the trail, you'll have grand views of Mount Washington, Black Butte, and other Central Cascade peaks.)

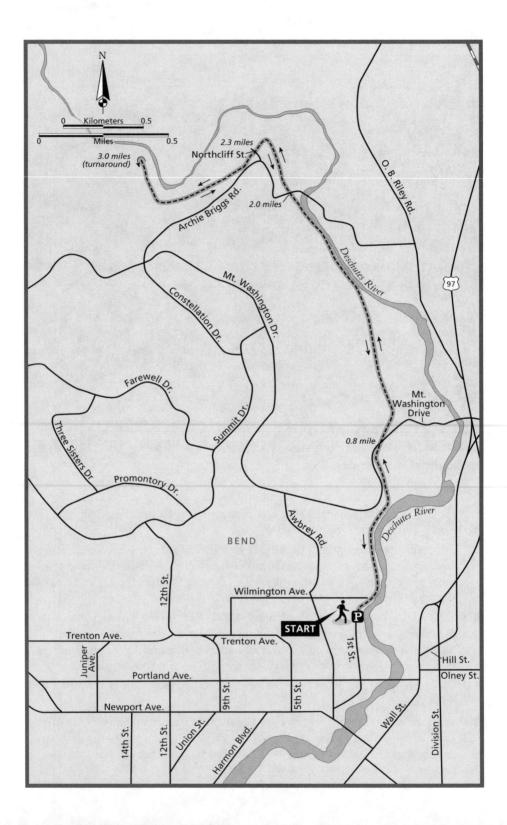

N

Kilometers
0   0.5
Miles
0   0.5

3.0 miles
(turnaround)

2.3 miles
Northcliff St.

2.0 miles

Archie Briggs Rd.

O. B. Riley Rd.

97

Deschutes River

Mt. Washington Dr.

Constellation Dr.

Farewell Dr.

Summit Dr.

Three Sisters Dr.

Promontory Dr.

Mt.
Washington
Drive

0.8 mile

Awbrey Rd.

Deschutes River

BEND

12th St.

Wilmington Ave.

START

1st St.

P

Trenton Ave.

Trenton Ave.

Hill St.

Juniper Ave.

Portland Ave.

Olney St.

9th St.

5th St.

Newport Ave.

14th St.

12th St.

Union St.

Harmon Blvd.

Wall St.

Division St.

3.0 Arrive at the route's turnaround point at the trail's end. Retrace the same route back to your starting point at First Street Rapids Park.

6.0 Arrive at the trailhead at First Street Rapids Park.

TRAIL FOOD

Alpenglow Café, 1040 Northwest Bond Street, Bend, OR 97701, (541) 383–7676
Café Sante, 718 Northwest Franklin Street, Bend, OR 97701, (541) 383–3530

55: Shevlin Park Loop

Region/area:	Bend
Pain:	2
Gain:	3
Distance:	4.9-mile loop
Elevation gain:	250 feet
Time:	45 minutes to 1 hour
The route:	Singletrack trail (with a small dose of doubletrack and paved road) that winds through a ponderosa pine forest in Shevlin Park. The ride has two bridge crossings over Tumalo Creek and a few boulder hops.
Trail surface:	95% smooth dirt, 5% rocky
Sun exposure:	45%
Runability:	100%
Season:	April through October
Other users:	Hikers, mountain bikers
Canine compatibility:	Leashed dogs permitted
Permits/fees:	None
Trail contact:	Bend Metro Park & Recreation District, Bend, OR, (541) 389–7275, www.bendparksandrec.org
Map:	USGS Bend (7.5' series)

Trail scoop: This fun creek run is a local's favorite and is only minutes from downtown Bend. The mostly singletrack route winds through ponderosa and Douglas fir forest along the banks of picturesque Tumalo Creek in Shevlin Park. No rest rooms or water are available at the trailhead.

Getting warmed up on the Shevlin Park Loop Trail

Finding the trailhead: From the intersection of Northwest Newport and Northwest 5th Street in downtown Bend, go 3.7 miles west on Northwest Newport Avenue (this turns into Shevlin Park Road after 1.9 miles) to the entrance to Shevlin Park. Turn left at the signed park entrance and park in the paved parking area by the wood trail sign. *DeLorme: Oregon Atlas & Gazetteer:* Page 51 C5.

TRAIL DIRT

0.0 From the paved parking area go around a metal gate. Start running on the singletrack trail that starts on the left side of a large wooden trail sign. (This section of the trail is virtually flat and takes you through a thick grove of aspens.)

0.1 Turn left and follow the singletrack trail for about 100 yards until you reach a wood bridge that crosses Tumalo Creek. Cross the bridge over the creek. After crossing the bridge turn right and follow the singletrack trail about 25 yards upstream. The trail then curves sharply to the left and switchbacks steeply uphill.

0.2 Turn right at the T intersection.

0.3 Turn right at the trail fork and continue cruising through a clear-cut area on a high ridge above the creek.

0.8 Turn left. (Ignore the spur trail that heads downhill to the creek.)

0.9 Turn right onto a doubletrack road.

1.2 Turn right onto a singletrack trail.

1.5 Watch for a large boulder in the trail.

1.9 Turn left and continue cruising on the singletrack trail along the ridge. (Ignore the singletrack trail that heads downhill to the right.)

2.0 Turn right onto a doubletrack road. (The route takes you downhill toward the creek. Then you'll cross over a drainage pipe and head uphill.)

2.1 Turn right onto a doubletrack road. Go about 25 yards and arrive at a T intersection. Turn left onto a singletrack trail.

2.5 Cross a narrow wood bridge over Tumalo Creek. After crossing the bridge continue on the singletrack trail as it heads downstream.

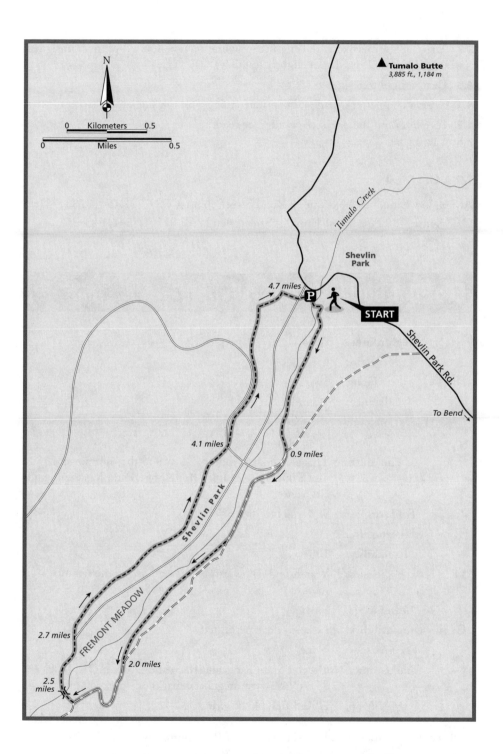

N

0   Kilometers   0.5

0   Miles   0.5

▲ **Tumalo Butte**
3,885 ft., 1,184 m

Tumalo Creek

**Shevlin
Park**

4.7 miles

P

START

Shevlin Park Rd.

To Bend

0.9 miles

4.1 miles

Shevlin Park

2.7 miles

FREMONT MEADOW

2.0 miles

*2.5
miles*

2.7 Arrive at a somewhat confusing five-way intersection. Go left onto an unsigned singletrack trail that heads slightly uphill.

4.0 Turn right onto a singletrack trail.

4.1 Cross a doubletrack road and continue cruising on the singletrack trail.

4.7 Turn left onto the paved park entrance road.

4.9 Arrive back at the trailhead.

TRAIL FOOD

Alpenglow Café, 1040 Northwest Bond Street, Bend, OR 97701, (541) 383–7676

Café Sante, 718 Northwest Franklin Street, Bend, OR 97701, (541) 383–3530

56: Pilot Butte State Park

Region/area:	Bend
Pain:	4
Gain:	3
Distance:	1.7 miles out and back
Elevation gain:	480 feet
Time:	20 to 30 minutes
The route:	This challenging route takes you to the summit of 4,138-foot Pilot Butte in Pilot Butte State Park. Mountain and city views.
Trail surface:	95% smooth dirt, 5% paved
Sun exposure:	100%
Runability:	100%
Season:	Year-round (snow can be present during the winter months)
Other users:	Hikers
Canine compatibility:	Leashed dogs permitted
Permits/fees:	None
Trail contact:	Oregon State Parks and Recreation, Salem OR, (800) 551–6949, www.oregonstateparks.org/park_42.php
Map:	USGS Bend (7.5' series)

Trail scoop: This route winds to the summit of Pilot Butte, giving you a 360-degree view of the surrounding high-desert country. You'll get an outstanding dirt track, a

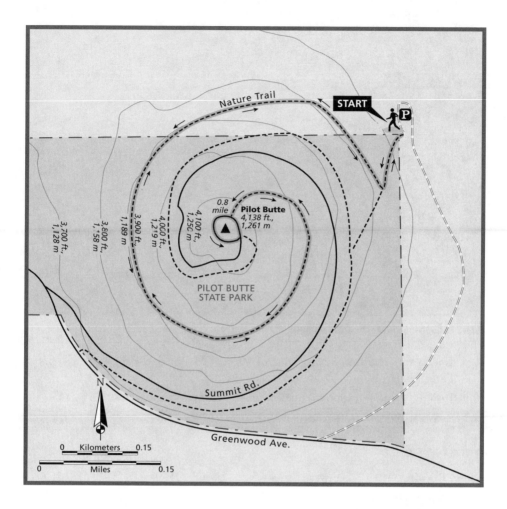

short intense cardio workout, and views of the gorgeous Central Cascade Mountains and city of Bend. A trail-run race is held annually at the top of this spectacular butte (contact information is under the month of September in the Race Calendar). Rest rooms are available at the trailhead. No water is available.

Finding the trailhead: From U.S. Highway 97 in Bend, turn east onto Greenwood Avenue. Go 1.5 miles and turn left at the Pilot Butte Trailhead sign. Continue to a large parking area at the trailhead. *DeLorme: Oregon Atlas & Gazetteer:* Page 51 D6.

TRAIL DIRT

0.0 Start running on the paved path adjacent to the parking area.

0.1 Turn right on the signed dirt nature trail. Power uphill on the smooth single-track trail that climbs to the 4,138-foot summit of Pilot Butte.

0.8 Turn right onto the paved summit road. Run around the summit circle and take

Central Cascade views from the summit of Pilot Butte

time to stop and soak in the gorgeous view of Mount Bachelor, Broken Top, the Three Sisters, Mount Washington, and other Central Cascade peaks.

0.9 Turn right and retrace the same route back to your starting point

1.7 Arrive at the trailhead.

TRAIL FOOD

Bend Brewing, 1019 Northwest Brooks Street, Bend, OR 97701, (541) 383–1599, www.sharplink.com/bbc

57: Deschutes River Trail

Region/area:	Bend
Pain:	2
Gain:	4
Distance:	4.4 miles out and back (or a 16.6-mile out-and-back option)
Elevation gain:	150 feet for 4.4-mile route (300 feet for the 16.6-mile route)
Time:	40 minutes to 1 hour for the 4.4-mile route; 4.25 to 5 hours for the 16.6-mile route
The route:	A beautiful river trail just outside Bend's city limits. Views.

Enjoying a run on the Deschutes River Trail

Trail surface:	75% smooth dirt, 25% rocky
Sun exposure:	35%
Runability:	100%
Season:	Year-round (snow may be present during the winter months)
Other users:	Hikers, mountain bikers, equestrians
Canine compatibility:	Leashed dogs permitted
Permits/fees:	No permits required if you start from the Meadow Picnic Area. All other Deschutes River trailheads require a $5.00 Northwest Forest Pass, purchased by calling (800) 270–7504, or online at www.naturenw.org.
Trail contact:	Deschutes National Forest, Bend, OR, (541) 383–5300, www.fs.fed.us/r6/centraloregon
Maps:	USGS Benham Falls (7.5' series); USFS *Deschutes River Trail* map, available online at www.fs.fed.us/r6/centraloregon

Trail scoop: The Deschutes River Trail is one of the premier running trails around Bend. It twists and turns along the lava-strewn Deschutes River past waterfalls, boiling rapids, and everything else in between. You'll see tons of wildlife as well as hikers, mountain bikers, and other runners on this very popular trail. Rest rooms are available at the trailhead (no water).

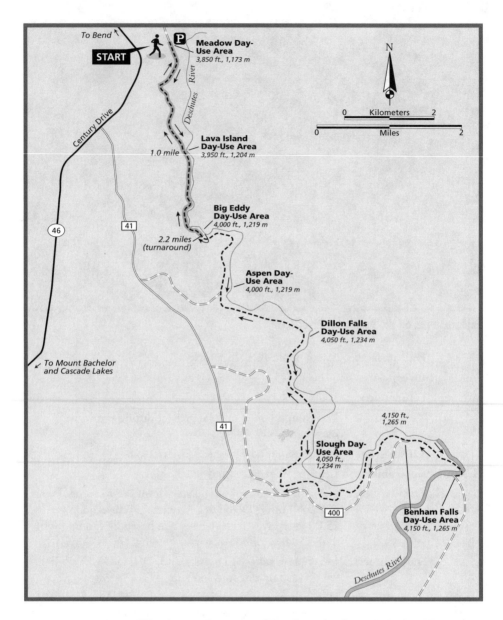

Finding the trailhead: Head 6.2 miles west of Bend on the Cascade Lakes Highway (Oregon Highway 46) and turn left onto the gravel Forest Service Road 100 at the MEADOW PICNIC AREA sign. Continue 1.4 miles to the parking area and trailhead. *DeLorme: Oregon Atlas & Gazetteer:* Page 45 A5.

TRAIL DIRT

0.0 Begin your journey at the wooden trail sign that states DESCHUTES RIVER
    TRAILS/LAVA ISLAND ROCK SHELTER 1/LAVA ISLAND FALLS 1.2/DILLON FALLS 4.5/

BENHAM FALLS 8.5. Follow the singletrack trail as it heads up a short hill and then winds around lava outcrops above the river through a gorgeous ponderosa pine forest.

0.5 Arrive at a large pond. Look for a small hiker symbol and take a sharp left. Follow the dirt path as it crosses the pond on a built-up dike. Continue on the trail as it follows the contours of the river.

1.0 Reach Lava Island Shelter. Go about 100 yards and keep following the main trail as it follows the riverbank.

2.2 Arrive at Big Eddy Rapids, your turnaround point. Retrace the same route back to the trailhead. (**Option:** If you crave more dirt, you can continue on to Benham Falls (west) Day Use Area and back to the Meadow Picnic Area for a total of 16.6 miles.)

4.4 Arrive at the trailhead.

TRAIL FOOD

Deschutes Brewery, 1044 Northwest Bond Street, Bend, OR 97701, (541) 382–9242, www.deschutesbrewery.com

58: Tumalo Falls

Region/area:	Bend
Pain:	2
Gain:	4
Distance:	7.6 miles out and back
Elevation gain:	200 feet
Time:	1.75 to 2.5 hours
The route:	A grand singletrack trail journeys through a sunny pine-scented forest, along the contours of Tumalo Creek, and to a spectacular viewpoint of Tumalo Falls.
Trail surface:	85% smooth dirt, 15% rocky
Sun exposure:	60%
Runability:	100%
Season:	May through November
Other users:	Hikers, mountain bikers, equestrians
Canine compatibility:	Dogs permitted

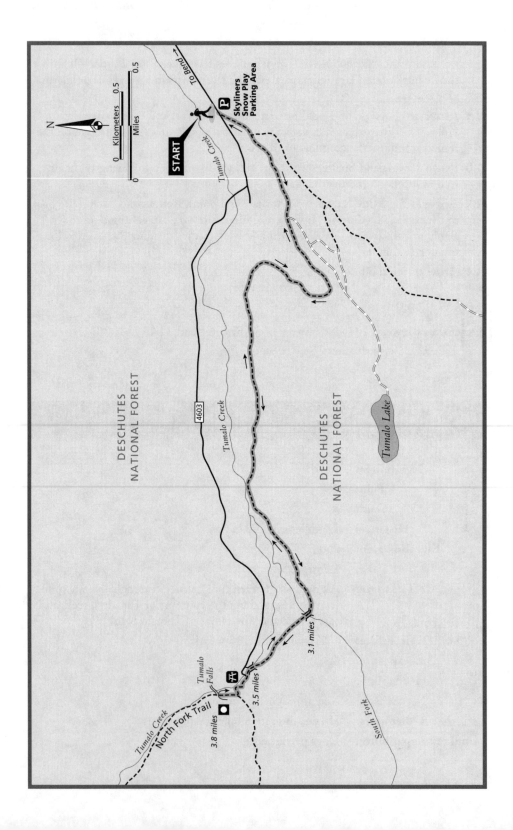

Permits/fees: $5.00 Northwest Forest Pass is required to park at the trailhead. You can purchase one by calling (800) 270–7504, or online at www.naturenw.org.

Trail contact: Deschutes National Forest, Bend, OR, (541) 383–5300, www.fs.fed.us/r6/centraloregon

Map: USGS Tumalo Falls (7.5' series)

Trail scoop: This fun route takes you uphill through a pine-scented forest, through loads of green-leafed manzanita and along the banks of Tumalo Creek. At the trail's halfway point, you'll get to soak in the gorgeous view of Tumalo Falls. After you check out the falls, put on your cruise control and sail downhill back to the trailhead. Rest rooms (no water) are available at the trailhead.

Finding the trailhead: From the intersection of Northwest Franklin and Highway 97 in Bend, turn west onto Franklin Avenue (this turns into Riverside Boulevard). Go 1.2 miles and turn right onto Tumalo Avenue. Continue on Tumalo Avenue (this road turns into Galveston Avenue and then Skyliners Road) for about 12 miles to the Skyliners Snow Play Parking Area on the left. *DeLorme: Oregon Atlas & Gazetteer:* Page 50 D4.

Tumalo Falls

TRAIL DIRT

0.0 Start running on the singletrack trail that begins next to the rest room.

0.1 Cross a doubletrack road and continue straight.

0.8 Turn right at the trail fork where a sign reads TUMALO FALLS. *(For the next 0.3 mile, you'll have to negotiate some rocky sections in the trail.)*

1.1 Continue straight (left) on the Tumalo Creek Trail.

3.1 Cross a footbridge.

3.2 Continue straight toward Tumalo Falls.

3.5 Cross a footbridge.

3.6 Arrive at a paved parking lot at the Tumalo Falls Picnic Area. Continue running on the North Fork Trail, which is adjacent to the large interpretive signs.

3.8 Arrive at a gorgeous viewpoint of Tumalo Falls. From here, retrace the same route back your starting point.

7.6 Arrive at the trailhead.

TRAIL FOOD

Bend Brewing, 1019 Northwest Brooks Street, Bend, OR 97701, (541) 383–1599, www.sharplink.com/bbc

Deschutes Brewery, 1044 Northwest Bond Street, Bend, OR 97701, (541) 382–9242, www.deschutesbrewery.com

59: Green Lakes Loop

Region/area:	Bend
Pain:	5
Gain:	5
Distance:	11.6-mile loop
Elevation gain:	1,175 feet
Time:	2.5 to 3.5 hours
The route:	This gorgeous (and very popular) route travels uphill paralleling enchanting Fall Creek and then enters the Green Lakes Basin. The return loop takes you on the Soda Creek Trail through more gorgeous Three Sisters Wilderness. Bridgeless creek crossings. Mountain views. Rest rooms (no water) are available at the trailhead.
Trail surface:	95% smooth dirt, 5% rocky
Sun exposure:	60%
Runability:	100%
Season:	Mid-June through October
Other users:	Hikers
Canine compatibility:	Leashed dogs permitted
Permits/fees:	$5.00 Northwest Forest Pass required to park at the trailhead. A free wilderness permit is also required. Self-issue permits are available at the trailhead.
Trail contact:	Deschutes National Forest, Bend, OR, (541) 383–5300, www.fs.fed.us/r6/centraloregon
Maps:	USGS Broken Top (7.5' series); Geo-Graphics Three Sisters Wilderness

Trail scoop: The initial 4 miles of this trail deliver gobs of beautiful creek scenery on brilliant dirt. You'll most likely be treading with many other high-spirited trail users, but the path is generally wide and passing is easy. Get psyched to charge up a couple of short steep sections before reaching the Green Lakes Basin. After 4 miles you'll leave the masses behind and wind up the southern flanks of Broken Top through gorgeous open country. Especially nice is the Green Lakes Basin, with the South Sister looming in the background. Head back on the Soda Creek Trail. Initially you'll dump some altitude, but the last couple of miles are on speed-inspiring flat sandy trail. Rest rooms (no water) are at the trailhead.

Finding the trailhead: From the intersection of U.S. Highway 97 and Franklin

On the Green Lakes Trail

Avenue in downtown Bend, turn west onto Franklin Avenue. Proceed 1.2 miles (Franklin Avenue turns into Riverside Boulevard) to the intersection with Tumalo Avenue. Turn right onto Tumalo Avenue (which turns into Galveston Avenue). Go 0.5 mile and turn left onto 14th Street. This street soon turns into Century Drive, also known as the Cascade Lakes Highway (OR Highway 46). Continue about 27 miles on the Cascade Lakes Highway to the Green Lakes Trailhead parking area on the right side of the road. *DeLorme: Oregon Atlas & Gazetteer:* Page 50 D3.

TRAIL DIRT

0.0 Start running on the smooth wide Trail #17 that parallels Fall Creek. A sign at the start of the trail indicates MORAINE LAKE 2 MILES/GREEN LAKES 4.5 MILES/PARK MEADOW 9 MILES/SCOTT PASS 21 MILES. (The route parallels Fall Creek, which has beautiful waterfalls around almost every bend.)

2.0 Arrive at a trail junction. Continue straight (right) on the smooth track as it parallels Fall Creek. (The trail that goes left at this junction heads toward Moraine Lake.)

4.3 Turn right toward Park Meadow/Soda Creek. Run 10 yards and then take another quick right turn toward Soda Creek/Broken Top. Continue climbing up the trail and enjoy awesome views of the Green Lakes to the north. The route skirts the south edge of the 9,175-foot Broken Top peak.

7.1 Turn right toward Soda Creek/Todd Lake. (The Broken Top Trail continues left at this junction.)

7.9 Turn right where a sign indicates Soda Creek. (The trail that goes left heads

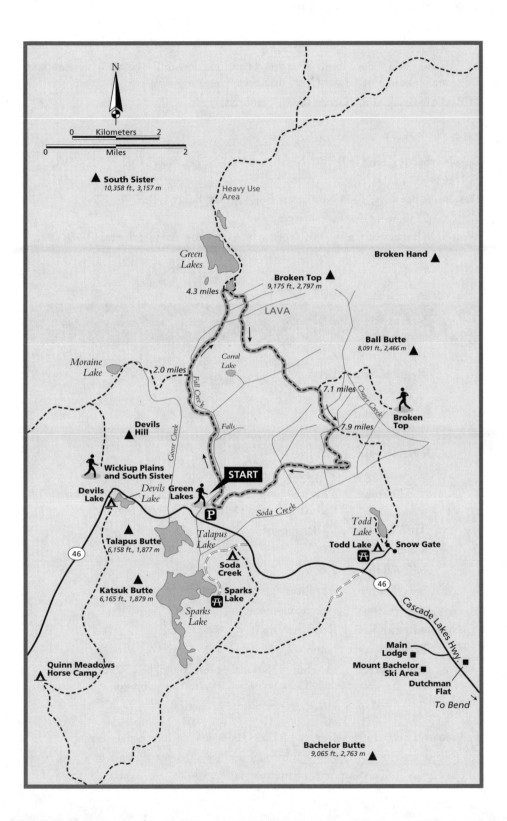

toward Todd Lake.) From here, you'll continue downhill—be ready to negotiate water crossings at Crater Creek and Soda Creek.

11.6 Arrive back at the Green Lakes Trailhead.

TRAIL FOOD

Baja Norte Mexican Grill, 801 Northwest Wall Street, Bend, OR 97701, (541) 593–9374

Deschutes Brewery, 1044 Northwest Bond Street, Bend, OR 97701, (541) 382–9242, www.deschutesbrewery.com

West Side Bakery & Café, 1005 Northwest Galveston Avenue, Bend, OR 97701, (541) 382–3426

60: Fall River

Region/area:	Bend
Pain:	1
Gain:	3
Distance:	6.4 miles out and back
Elevation gain:	100 feet
Time:	1 to 1.25 hours
The route:	This trail loop takes you along the crystal-clear waters of Fall River in the Deschutes National Forest.
Trail surface:	100% smooth dirt
Sun exposure:	10%
Runability:	100%
Season:	April through November
Other users:	Hikers, mountain bikers
Canine compatibility:	Dogs permitted
Permits/fees:	None
Trail contact:	Deschutes National Forest, Bend, OR 97701, (541) 383–5300, www.fs.fed.us/r6/centraloregon
Map:	USGS Pistol Butte (7.5' series)

Trail scoop: This beautiful river trail follows the course of the crystal-clear, spring-fed Fall River. This route takes you through immense groves of ponderosa pine trees and has many scenic viewpoints of the river where you may see Canada Geese, osprey, and mallard ducks. No rest rooms or water are available at the trailhead.

Finding the trailhead: From the intersection of Greenwood Avenue and U.S. Highway 97 in Bend, travel 16.7 miles south on U.S. Highway 97. Turn right (west) onto Vandevert Road at the VANDEVERT ROAD/FALL RIVER sign. Continue 1 mile on Vandevert Road to the junction with South Century Drive. Turn left onto South Century Drive and go 1 mile to the junction with Cascade Lakes Highway (Forest Service Road 42). Turn right (west) and continue 10.4 miles (you'll pass Fall River Campground on the left after 9.7 miles) on the Cascade Lakes Highway

Wildlife on the Fall River Trail

to an unsigned gravel circular parking area on the left side of the road. A green forest-service building is also located adjacent to the parking area. *DeLorme: Oregon Atlas & Gazetteer:* Page 44 B3

TRAIL DIRT

0.0 Start the run on a doubletrack road that begins adjacent to a wood pole fence. The doubletrack road heads east and follows Fall River downstream. Go 75 yards and veer left onto a smaller doubletrack road. (This road soon turns into a wide singletrack trail that takes you through a corridor of old-growth ponderosa pine trees.)

0.5 Arrive at a sign (facing the other way) that states END OF TRAIL/PARKING ON ROAD 42. Ignore the sign and continue cruising east as the trail parallels Fall River.

0.6 Veer right at the brown hiker sign. Just past this junction you'll pass a picturesque wood bridge that spans Fall Creek.

0.7 Arrive at Fall Creek Campground Day-Use Area. (Rest rooms are available on your left.) Hook up with the gravel campground loop road and continue running east to the far end of the campground.

0.8 Veer right onto the unsigned singletrack Fall River Trail that begins just to the left of campsite #8. The trail continues to weave through a thick lodgepole pine forest right near the river's edge.

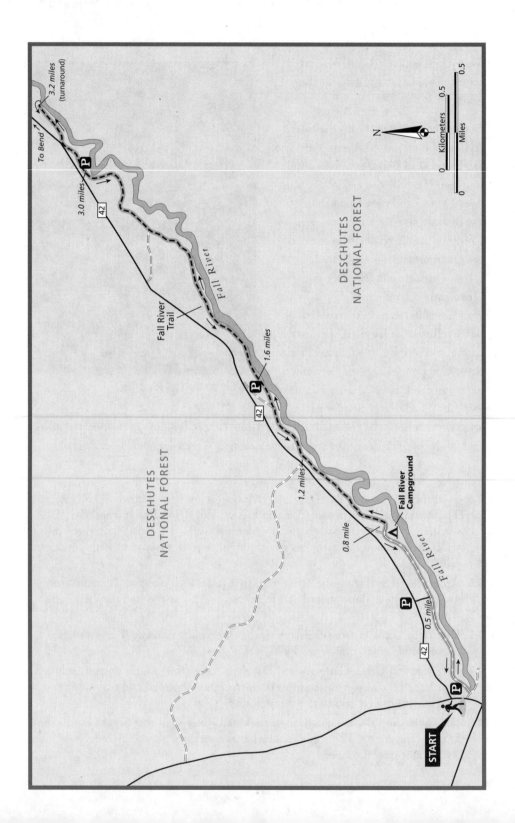

DESCHUTES NATIONAL FOREST

DESCHUTES NATIONAL FOREST

To Bend →

3.2 miles (turnaround)

3.0 miles

42

Fall River Trail

Fall River

1.6 miles

42

1.2 miles

0.8 mile

Fall River Campground

Fall River

0.5 mile

42

START

N

Kilometers 0.5

0   0.5

Miles

1.2 The trail intersects a red-cinder road. Turn right onto the cinder road and continue east for 0.3 mile.

1.5 Turn right onto an unsigned doubletrack road.

1.6 Take a sharp right and continue sailing on the unsigned singletrack trail that dips in and out of an area thick with fallen logs.

3.0 Arrive in a red-cinder parking area. Continue straight across the parking area and continue on the signed Fall River Trail.

3.2 Arrive at the trail's ending point, a rock dam where a sign says END OF TRAIL. Retrace the same route back to your starting point.

6.4 Arrive at the trailhead.

TRAIL FOOD

Bend Brewing Company, 1019 Northwest Brooks Street, Bend, OR 97701, (541) 383–1599

Deschutes Brewery, 1044 Northwest Bond Street, Bend, OR 97701, (541) 382–9242, www.deschutesbrewery.com

61: Paulina Lake Loop

Region/area:	Bend
Pain:	3
Gain:	4
Distance:	7.5-mile loop
Elevation gain:	230 feet
Time:	2 to 3 hours
The route:	This trail loops around scenic Paulina Lake in the Newberry National Volcanic Monument. Mountain views.
Trail surface:	65% smooth dirt, 35% rocky
Sun exposure:	65%
Runability:	100%
Season:	Year-round
Other users:	Hikers
Canine compatibility:	Leashed dogs permitted
Permits/fees:	$5.00 Northwest Forest Pass, purchased by calling (800) 270–7504, or online at www.naturenw.org.

Finding solitude on the Paulina Lakeshore Trail

Trail contact:	Newberry National Volcanic Monument, Deschutes National Forest, Bend, OR, (541) 383–5300, www.fs. fed.us/r6/centraloregon/index-monument.html
Map:	USGS Paulina Peak (7.5' series)

Trail scoop: Get jazzed to run on sweet singletrack around Paulina Lake in the gorgeous Newberry National Volcanic Monument. This high-alpine run takes you past prime swimming beaches, piles of shiny black obsidian, and stellar views of 7,984-foot Paulina Peak. Bring bug juice—the mosquitoes can be fierce in the spring and summer. Rest rooms and water are available at the trailhead.

Finding the trailhead: From the intersection of Franklin Avenue in Bend, travel 23 miles south on U.S. Highway 97. Turn left (east) onto Forest Service Road 21 (Paulina Lake Road). After 11.6 miles you'll pass the entrance booth to the national monument on your left. Continue 1.6 miles past the entrance booth to the Paulina Lake Trailhead on the left.

TRAIL DIRT

0.0 From the paved parking area, start around the lake in a counterclockwise direction on the signed Paulina Lakeshore Trail. The trail starts out as a gravel path lined with stones.

0.1 Run across a paved boat ramp and continue running on the signed trail. Not far past this junction a sign indicates LITTLE CRATER CAMPGROUND 2.5 MILES.

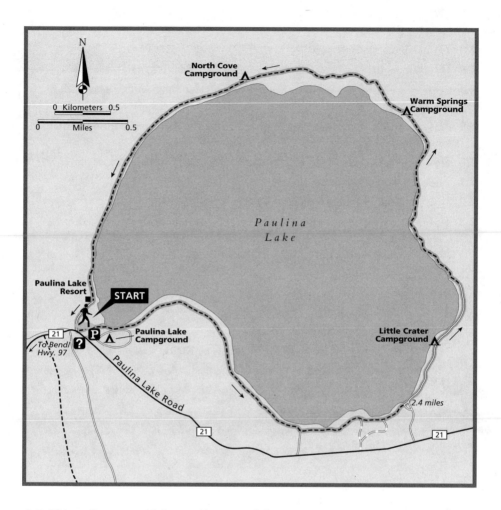

1.5 The trail seems to fade out. Continue following the lakeshore.

1.7 The trail is evident again and turns into a long grassy track next to an inviting sandy beach.

2.2 Arrive at a paved boat ramp that has a rest room and picnic tables. After crossing the paved boat ramp you'll arrive at a sign that states PAULINA LAKESHORE LOOP TRAIL/TRAIL FOLLOWS ROAD. (From this point you'll follow the paved road as it parallels the lakeshore.)

2.4 Arrive at the entrance to Little Crater Campground. Continue on the paved road through the campground as it follows the lakeshore.

2.5 Pass a rest room and a water faucet. Follow the road through the campground until it ends. Turn right into a gravel trailhead parking lot and pick up the Paulina Lakeshore Trail. There are two trails at this parking area. Take the trail going left. *(The trail goes around a rocky point with cool lava outcroppings and fantastic views of Paulina Peak. Watch your footing over the next mile—it is rocky and filled with tree roots.)*

4.0 Turn right at the trail sign.

4.5 The trail begins climbing a high ridge above the lake for the next 0.5 mile.

5.0 Begin descending the ridge on a series of long sweeping switchbacks back to the lakeshore.

6.9 Pass several vacation cabins on your right. The trail becomes faint here. Keep following the lakeshore.

7.0 Turn right on a gravel road next to the Paulina Lake Resort general store.

7.1 The road turns to pavement.

7.2 Turn left onto the unsigned dirt singletrack trail.

7.3 Turn left onto a paved road and then cross a concrete bridge over Paulina Creek. Immediately after crossing the bridge, turn left, go down a set of stone steps, and pick up the unsigned dirt trail.

7.5 Arrive at the trailhead.

Geology 101

Paulina Peak rises 7,984 feet above Paulina Lake and is what remains of ancient Mount Newberry, which, at 10,000 feet, was once the highest volcano in the Paulina Mountains. About 200,000 years ago, Newberry erupted and collapsed. The huge caldera left in its place eventually filled with water to create an enormous lake. Thousands of years later, more eruptions split the water into two separate lakes (Paulina and East) and left a central cone and several obsidian flows.

TRAIL FOOD

Bend Brewing Company, 1019 Northwest Brooks Street, Bend, OR 97701, (541) 383–1599

Deschutes Brewery, 1044 Northwest Bond Street, Bend, OR 97701, (541) 382–9242, www.deschutesbrewery.com

Oregon Coast

Oregon's magical coastline is filled with trails that have phenomenal views of the rugged, rocky coast and pounding surf. The Oregon Coast is separated from the rest of Oregon by the north-south-running Coast Range Mountains, which are covered with a patchwork of deep green cedar and fir forest. Flowing from these mountains are coastal rivers that flow into scenic bays and estuaries. If you want to run through a beautiful coastal forest to a scenic viewpoint where you may spot gray whales, check out the Cape Lookout Trail. If you want to run for miles on a long sandy beach next to the pounding surf, be sure to explore the Cannon Beach and Cape Kiwanda routes.

Region/area:	Oregon Coast
Pain:	2
Gain:	3
Distance:	3 miles out and back
Elevation gain:	400 feet
Time:	30 to 40 minutes
The route:	This trail begins in Ecola State Park and takes you through a beautiful coastal forest to Indian Beach. Views.
Trail surface:	90% smooth dirt, 10% rocky
Sun exposure:	10%
Runability:	100%
Season:	Year-round (can be very muddy during the winter months)
Other users:	Hikers
Canine compatibility:	Leashed dogs permitted
Permits/fees:	$3.00 Oregon State Park fee, payable at the park's entrance booth.
Trail contact:	Oregon State Parks and Recreation, Salem OR, (800) 551–6949, www.oregonstateparks.org/park_188.php
Map:	USGS Tillamook Head (7.5' series)

Trail scoop: This classic coastal route offers just about everything: a winding single-

Enjoying a run through a cool, coastal forest in Ecola State Park

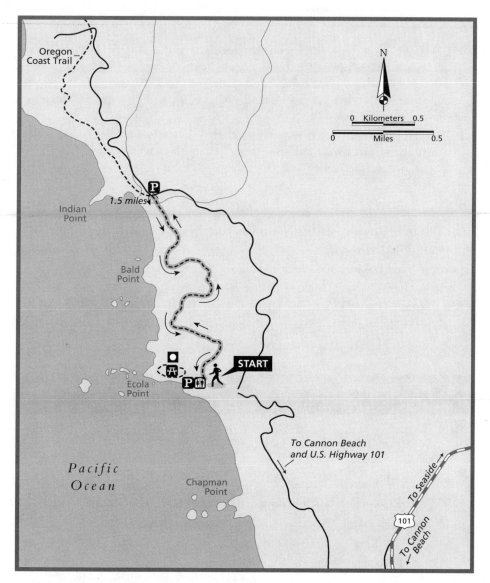

track trail through an immense coastal forest, awesome ocean views, and a picturesque beach. If you run this trail in the winter, get ready for a mud fest. Rest rooms
and water are available at the trailhead.

Finding the trailhead: From U.S. 101 at the north end of Cannon Beach, exit west at
the ECOLA STATE PARK sign. Travel about 0.25 mile and turn right at a small sign for
the park. Go 2.3 miles on a narrow, windy road to a large parking area and the trailhead. *DeLorme: Oregon Atlas & Gazetteer:* Page 64 A1.

TRAIL DIRT

0.0 Look for a small trailhead sign on the north side of the parking lot. Pick up the singletrack trail as it winds through a dense forest. Mossy covered logs and a fern-filled understory create a mystical quality to this alluring dirt track. (As the trail route heads north toward Indian Beach, you'll pass by spectacular cliff-side viewpoints of the ocean.)

1.5 Turn left at the fork that takes you to secluded Indian Beach (your turnaround point). From here, retrace the same route back to the starting point.

3.0 Arrive at the trailhead.

TRAIL FOOD

Bill's Tavern & Brewhouse, 188 North Hemlock Street, Cannon Beach, OR 97110, (503) 436–2202

Grain and Sand Baking, 1064 South Hemlock Street, Cannon Beach, OR 97110, (503) 436–0120

Pizza a' fetta, 231 North Hemlock Street, Cannon Beach, OR 97110, (503) 436–0333

63: Cannon Beach

Region/area:	Oregon Coast
Pain:	1
Gain:	3
Distance:	4.4 miles out and back (with longer options)
Elevation gain:	None
Time:	40 to 60 minutes
The route:	This beach route begins in downtown Cannon Beach and heads south past Haystack Rock to the Tolovana Beach Wayside. Views.
Trail surface:	95% sand, 5% paved
Sun exposure:	100%
Runability:	100%
Season:	Year-round
Other users:	Hikers
Canine compatibility:	Leashed dogs permitted
Permits/fees:	None

Haystack Rock at Cannon Beach

Trail contact: Cannon Beach Chamber of Commerce, Cannon Beach, OR, (503) 436–2623, www.cannonbeach.org

Map: USGS Tillamook Head (7.5' series)

Trail scoop: This classic coastal route packs in fresh Pacific air, a flat sandy beach, a fantastic ocean view, and a chance to view broods of squawking seabirds on 235-foot Haystack Rock. You'll get a good workout churning on packed sand, with the option of going on a longer route if you're feeling the need to lay more tracks. Crowds on nice weekends, storm gales with blowing sand, and awesome sand castles are some of the possible encounters on this beach trek. Rest rooms and water are available at the trailhead. (**Special considerations:** If you plan on running out to Hug Point, be sure to check the tide tables before departing.)

Finding the trailhead: Head about 73 miles west of Portland on U.S. Highway 26 to the intersection with U.S. Highway 101. Turn south onto U.S. Highway 101 and take the Cannon Beach exit. Continue driving south through downtown Cannon Beach to a public parking area located at the intersection of 2nd Street and Spruce Street. *DeLorme: Oregon Atlas & Gazetteer:* Page 64 A1.

TRAIL DIRT

0.0 From the public parking area, turn left onto Spruce Street.

0.1 Turn left onto 1st Street.

0.2 Cross Hemlock Street and continue west toward the beach. Cross Laurel Street

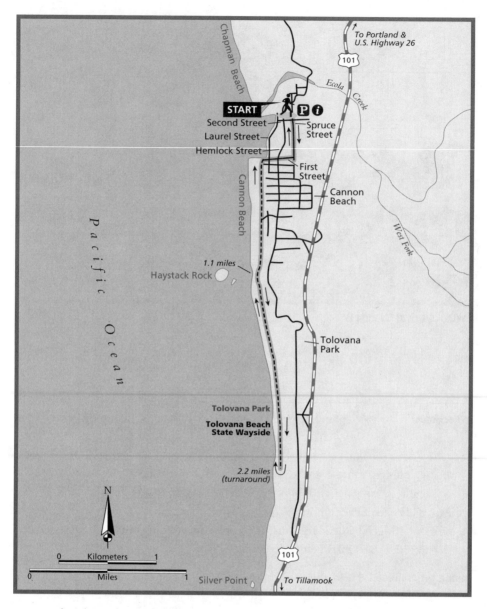

and pick up the sandy path that takes you to the beach. Once you reach the beach, turn left (south) and enjoy a fun trek on the long, flat sandy beach.

1.1 Pass 235-foot Haystack Rock on your right. From here, keep heading south.

2.2 Arrive at Tolovana Wayside (your turnaround point). Retrace the same route back to your starting point. (**Option:** Continue south for 3 more miles to Hug Point. If you plan on completing a longer route, check the tide tables and plan your run at low tide.)

4.4 Arrive at the public parking area and your starting point.

TRAIL FOOD

Bill's Tavern & Brewhouse, 188 North Hemlock Street, Cannon Beach, OR 97110, (503) 436–2202

Grain and Sand Baking, 1064 South Hemlock Street, Cannon Beach, OR 97110, (503) 436–0120

Pizza a' fetta, 231 North Hemlock Street, Cannon Beach, OR 97110, (503) 436–0333

64: Cape Lookout

Region/area:	Oregon Coast
Pain:	3
Gain:	3
Distance:	5 miles out and back
Elevation gain:	400 feet
Time:	1.25 to 1.5 hours
The route:	A classic coast trail that takes you through an amazing Sitka spruce forest to the tip of Cape Lookout. Views.
Trail surface:	95% smooth dirt, 5% rocky
Sun exposure:	10%
Runability:	100%
Season:	Year-round (the trail can be very muddy during the winter months)
Other users:	Hikers
Canine compatibility:	Leashed dogs permitted
Permits/fees:	$3.00 day-use fee
Trail contact:	Oregon State Parks and Recreation, Salem OR, (800) 551–6949, www.oregonstateparks.org/park_186.php
Map:	USGS Sand Lake (7.5' series)

Trail scoop: This coastal running adventure begins by switchbacking steeply downhill through a thick Sitka spruce forest. Distant views of Cape Kiwanda and Cascade Head to the south are a trail distraction you'll find just past 0.5 mile. Views looking north of Cape Meares and Neahkahnie Mountain begin at about 1.2 miles. The potentially slick wood boardwalks keep you up and out of the thick mire of mud that is present on this trail in the winter months. After 2.5 miles you'll reach the

One of the many spectacular ocean views on the Cape Lookout Trail

end of the trail at a spectacular viewpoint 400 feet from the crashing waves below. From this cliff-top viewpoint, look for the distant spray of migrating whales from December through June. No rest rooms or water are available at the trailhead.

Finding the trailhead: From U.S. Highway 101 in Tillamook, head 15.5 miles southwest on the Three Capes Scenic Highway to the signed Cape Lookout trailhead on the right side of the highway.

From the intersection of Highway 18 and U.S. Highway 101 in Lincoln City, turn north onto U.S. Highway 101. Travel 14.6 miles and turn left (west) onto Brooten Road where a sign states CAPE KIWANDA RECREATION AREA/PACIFIC CITY. Go 2.8 miles and turn left onto Pacific Avenue toward Netarts/Oceanside. Continue 0.3 mile and turn right onto Kiwanda Drive. Continue 15.3 miles north to the signed Cape Lookout trailhead on the left side of the highway. *DeLorme: Oregon Atlas & Gazetteer:* Page 58 B1.

TRAIL DIRT

0.0 Look for the trailhead in the southwest corner of the parking lot. Start running on the trail that heads left. Go 100 yards and stay to the right at the trail junction. (The trail sails downhill on a series of long switchbacks through a shady Sitka spruce forest.)

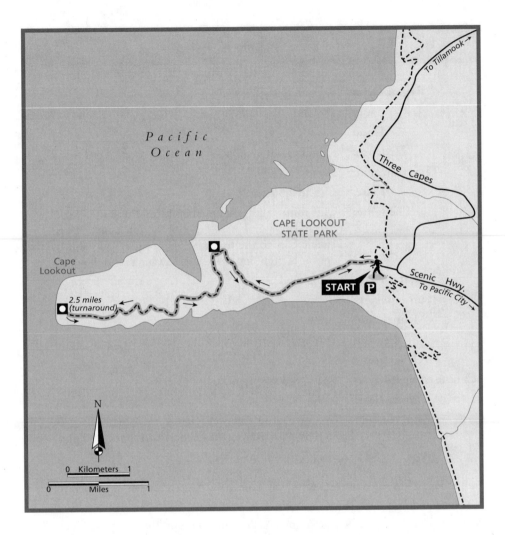

2.5 Arrive at a cliff-top viewpoint 400 feet above the waves below you. Enjoy the view then retrace the same route back to your starting point.

5.0 Arrive at the trailhead.

TRAIL FOOD

Grateful Bread Bakery, 34805 Brooten Road, Pacific City, OR (503) 965–7337

La Mexicana Restaurant, 2203 3rd Street, Tillamook, OR, (503) 842–2101

Pelican Public & Brewery, 33180 Cape Kiwanda Drive, Pacific City, OR 97135, (503) 965–7007, www.pelicanbrewery.com

65: Cape Kiwanda

Region/area:	Oregon Coast
Pain:	2
Gain:	4
Distance:	8.2 miles out and back
Elevation gain:	None
Time:	1.75 to 2.5 hours
The route:	This route takes you on a beach run through Cape Kiwanda Natural Area and Bob Straub State Park in Pacific City to the tip of Nestucca Spit. You also have the option of climbing the Cape Kiwanda sand dune. Views.
Trail surface:	100% sand
Sun exposure:	100%
Runability:	100%
Season:	Year-round
Other users:	Hikers
Canine compatibility:	Leashed dogs permitted
Permits/fees:	None
Trail contact:	Oregon State Parks and Recreation, Salem, OR, (800) 551–6949, www.oregonstateparks.org/park_180.php
Map:	USGS Nestucca Bay (7.5' series)

Trail scoop: This gorgeous beach run starts near the golden sandstone cliffs of Cape Kiwanda and Haystack Rock in Pacific City and heads south through Bob Straub State Park to the tip of Nestucca Spit. As you run south on the beach, you'll enjoy watching surfers and boogie boarders catching waves offshore and dory boats heading out into the surf to catch fish off Haystack Rock. If you still have energy left to burn after your run, head north from the parking area and climb to the top of the Cape Kiwanda sand dune. The views from the top are gorgeous and running down the dune is a blast. Rest rooms and water are available at the parking area.

Finding the trailhead: From the intersection of Highway 18 and U.S. Highway 101 in Lincoln City, turn north onto U.S. Highway 101. Travel 14.6 miles and turn left (west) onto Brooten Road where a sign states CAPE KIWANDA RECREATION AREA/ PACIFIC CITY. Go 2.8 miles and turn left onto Pacific Avenue toward Netarts/ Oceanside. Continue 0.3 mile and turn right onto Kiwanda Drive. Go 1 mile and turn left into the Cape Kiwanda public parking area adjacent to the Pelican Pub and Brewery Restaurant.

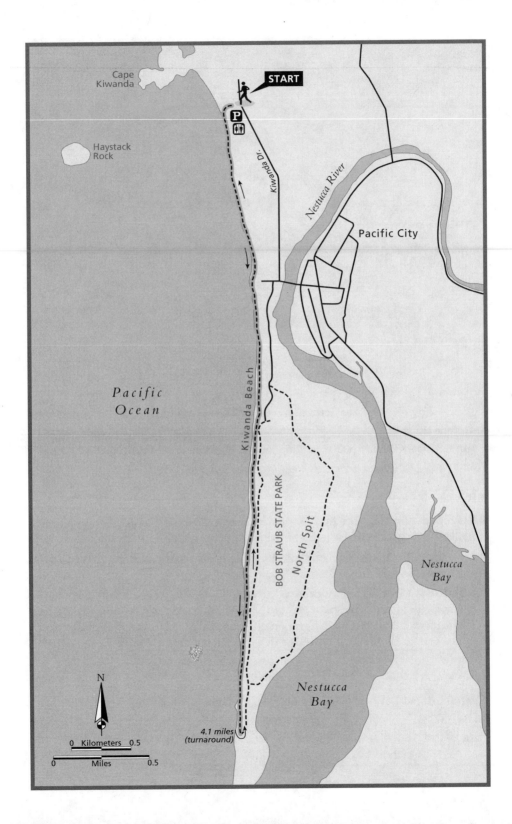

START

Cape
Kiwanda

Haystack
Rock

*Pacific
Ocean*

Kiwanda Dr.

Nestucca River

Pacific City

Kiwanda Beach

BOB STRAUB STATE PARK

North Spit

*Nestucca
Bay*

*Nestucca
Bay*

N

0   Kilometers   0.5

0   Miles   0.5

4.1 miles
(turnaround)

Gorgeous Cape Kiwanda

From Tillamook travel 25 miles south on U.S. Highway 101 and turn right (west) onto Brooten Road at the CAPE KIWANDA RECREATION AREA/PACIFIC CITY sign. Go 2.8 miles and turn left onto Pacific Avenue toward Netarts/Oceanside. Continue 0.3 mile and turn right onto Kiwanda Drive. Go 1 mile and then turn left into the Cape Kiwanda public parking area adjacent to the Pelican Pub and Brewery Restaurant. *DeLorme: Oregon Atlas & Gazetteer:* Page 58 C1.

TRAIL DIRT

0.0 From the parking area, head out to the beach. Turn left (south) and run on the flat, sandy beach for 4.1 miles to the tip of Nestucca Spit.

4.1 Arrive at the tip of Nestucca Spit. From here, retrace the same route back to your starting point.

8.2 Arrive at the trailhead. **(Option:** Be sure to climb the great sand dune known as Cape Kiwanda on the south end of the beach. It's not runable going up. So, to effectively climb this mastiff, get on all fours and use your hands as blades to make progress. Coming down is a definite run with no consequence of falling!)

TRAIL FOOD

Grateful Bread Bakery, 34805 Brooten Road, Pacific City, OR 97135, (503) 965–7337

Pelican Public & Brewery, 33180 Cape Kiwanda Drive, Pacific City, OR 97135, (503) 965–7007, www.pelicanbrewery.com

Resources

General Information

Bend Metro Park & Recreation District, 200 Northwest Pacific Park Lane, Bend, OR 97701, (541) 389–7275, www.bendparksandrec.org

Cannon Beach Chamber of Commerce, 207 North Spruce Street, Cannon Beach, OR 97110, (503) 436–2623, www.cannonbeach.org

Columbia River Gorge National Scenic Area, 902 Wasco Avenue, Suite 200, Hood River, OR 97031, (541) 386–2333, www.fs.fed.us/r6/columbia

Crooked River National Grassland, 813 Southwest Highway 97, Madras, OR 97741, (541) 475–9272, www.fs.fed.us/r6/centraloregon/manageinfo/nepa/sop/ochcrook.html

Deschutes National Forest, 1645 Highway 20 East, Bend, OR 97701, (541) 383–5300, www.fs.fed.us/r6/centraloregon

Estacada Ranger Station, Mount Hood National Forest, 595 Northwest Industrial Way, Estacada, OR 97023, (503) 630–8700, www.fs.fed.us/r6/mthood

Eugene Parks, 1820 Roosevelt Boulevard, Eugene, OR 97401, (541) 682–4800, www.ci.eugene.or.us/PW/PARKS/index.htm

John Day Fossil Beds National Monument HCR 82, Box 126, Kimberly, OR 97848-9701, (541) 987–2333, www.nps.gov/joda

Lane County Parks, 90064 Coburg Road, Eugene, OR 97408, (541) 682–4414, www.co.lane.or.us/parks/laneParks.htm

McKenzie Ranger District, Willamette National Forest, 57600 McKenzie Highway, McKenzie Bridge, OR 97413, (541) 822–3381, www.fs.fed.us/r6/willamette

Middle Fork Ranger District, Willamette National Forest, Lowell Office, 60 South Pioneer Street, Lowell, OR 97452, (541) 937–2129, www.fs.fed.us/r6/willamette

Mount Hood National Forest Headquarters Office, 16400 Champion Way, Sandy, OR 97055, (503) 622–7674, www.fs.fed.us/r6/mthood

Newberry National Volcanic Monument, Deschutes National Forest, 1645 Highway 20 East, Bend, OR 97701, (541) 383–5300, www.fs.fed.us/r6/centraloregon/index-monument.html

Ochoco National Forest, 3160 Northeast 3rd Street, Prineville, OR 97754, (541) 416–6500, www.fs.fed.us/r6/centraloregon

Oregon Department of Fish and Wildlife, Sauvie Island Wildlife Area, 18330 Northwest Sauvie Island Road, Portland, OR 97231, (503) 621–3488, www.dfw.state.or.us

Oregon State Parks and Recreation, Suite 1, 1115 Commercial Street Northeast, Salem, OR 97301-1002, (800) 551–6949, www.oregonstateparks.org

Oregon State University, College of Forests, 8692 Peavey Arboretum Road, Corvallis, OR 97330, (541) 737–6702 or (541) 737–4434 (recorded message), www.cof.orst.edu/resfor/rec/purpose.sht

Portland Parks & Recreation, 1120 Southwest Fifth Avenue, Suite 1302, Portland, OR 97204, (503) 823–PLAY, www.parks.ci.portland.or.us

Sisters Ranger District, Deschutes National Forest, P.O. Box 249, Sisters, OR 97759, (541) 549–7700, www.fs.fed.us/r6/centraloregon

Running Clubs

Central Oregon Running Klub
P.O. Box 415
Bend, OR 97709
(541) 317–1882

Coast Hills Running Club
1215 Northeast Lakewood Drive
Newport, OR 97365
(541) 265–5738

Oregon Road Runners Club
4840 Southwest Western Avenue, #200
Beaverton, OR 97005
(503) 646–RUNR
www.orrc.net
orrc@orrc.net

The Good Race, Inc.
P.O. Box 480
Springfield, OR 97477
(541) 744–1042
www.goodrace.com

Willamette Valley Road Runners
P.O. Box 4002
Salem, Oregon 97302–1002
(503) 566–6708
www.wvroadrunners.org

Web Sites

www.altrec.com/shop/dir/trailrunning: Shopping site for trail runners. Contains trail-running gear as well as articles and links on skills and where to trail run.

www.bigredlizard.com: Contains race information and links for running, multisport events, and cycling.

www.racecenter.com: Promotes all types of running events in the Northwest. It includes online entry forms, race results, and training tips.

www.orcc.com: Oregon Road Running Club; contains information on races in Oregon and a group-training calendar.

www.portlandrunner.com: Portland's running resource, including running events, Portland running news, and links.

www.runoregon.com: Online forum of Oregon running events and happenings.

www.runtheplanet.com: Claims to be the world's largest running resource on the Web.

www.trailrunner.com: Official Web site for The American Trail Running Association, which supports trail running and mountain running.

Ultrarunner.net: Contains information about ultrarunning races and links to other ultrarunning sites.

Magazines

Northwest Runner (www.Northwestrunner.com)
Trail Runner (www.trailrunnermag.com)
Running Times (www.runningtimes.com)
Runner's World (www.runnersworld.com)
UltraRunning (www.ultrarunning.com/subscribe.htm)

Race Calendar

JANUARY
MLK Ultra (50K)
Lowell, OR
(541) 689–8335
ultrawillow@uswest.net

FEBRUARY
Hagg Lake Trail Run (50K)
Forest Grove, OR
(503) 642–0804
www.scottdiamond.com/Running/
races/HaggLake
hagglakerun@aol.com

Jack Frost 5-Hour Foot Race
Mary S. Young State Park
West Linn, OR
(503) 497–4080
www.bigredlizard.com

Wilsonville Wild Trail Run (8K)
Wilsonville Memorial Park
Wilsonville, OR
(503) 694–2877
www.bigredlizard.com

MARCH
Chuckanut Mountain (50K)
Bellingham, WA
(360) 398–1373
mwest@uswest.net

APRIL
McDonald Forest (15K, 50K)
Corvallis, OR
(541) 758–8124
www.orst.edu/groups/triclub/
ultramacultra@proaxis.com

Race for the Roses (5K)
AA Sports Ltd.
4840 Southwest Western Avenue,
Suite 400
Beaverton, OR 97005
(503) 531–3140
www.racecenter.com
aasports@racecenter.com

MAY
Mustang Madness Run (5K)
Sherwood, OR
(503) 925–1992
tstoner5@juno.com

Tillamook Burn Scramble (6 miles)
Timber, OR
(503) 497–4080
www.bigredlizard.com

JUNE
Columbia River Gorge Marathon and
Half-Marathon
Hood River, OR
(800) 828–7873
www.gorgemarathon.com

Mount Hood Scramble (6 miles)
Mount Hood, OR
(503) 497–4080
www.bigredlizard.com

Newport Marathon
1215 Northeast Lakewood Avenue
Newport, OR 97365
(541) 265–3446
www.newportmarathon.org
run@newportmarathon.org

Pacific Crest Half Ironman Triathlon
Sunriver, OR
(503) 531–3140
www.racecenter.com
aasports@racenter.com

Run for the Mountain (5K)
Mount Pisgah Arboretum
Eugene, OR
(541) 682–2000
www.racecenter.com
laneparks@co.lane.or.us

Starlight Run
Portland, OR
(503) 203–9166
www.ontherun.com/starlight

Winterhawk 6-Hour Trail Run
Forest Park
Portland, OR
(503) 669–2568
www.nothingtosay.com/redrun
redrunz@juno.com

JULY
Gorge Games Trail Run (10K & Half
Marathon)
Hood River, OR
(541) 386–7774
www.gorgegames.com

McCubbin's Gulch Scramble
McCubbin's Recreation Area
Mount Hood, OR
(503) 497–4080
www.bigredlizard.com

Siskiyou Outback Trail Run (15K &
50K)
P.O. Box 903
Ashland, OR 97520
(541) 488–2453
sob@danabandy.com

Super X Trail Run (5 miles)
Flying M Ranch
Yamhill, OR
(503) 662–3222
www.bigredlizard.com

AUGUST
Bend Marathon and 5-mile Trail Run
Bend Distillery
1470 Northeast 1st Street, #800
Bend, OR 97701
(541) 318–0200
www.bendistillery.com

Mount Hood Pacific Crest Trail
Ultramarathon (50K)
Mount Hood, OR
(503) 439–0799
www.scottdiamond.com/running/races/
pct/index.htm
michael.burke@portland.af.mil

Ski Bowl Scramble
Ski Bowl Resort
Mount Hood, OR
(503) 497–4080
www.bigredlizard.com

SEPTEMBER
McKenzie River Trail Run (50K)
5915 F Street
Springfield, OR
(541) 726–6203

www.users.uswest.net/~ultrawillow/
McKenzieRiver.html
phvaughn@mindspring.com

Race for the Cure (5K)
Portland, OR
(503) 553–3680
www.racteforthecure-pdx.org

Peak to Port Relay (60 Miles—Mary's
Peak to Yaquina Bay in Newport)
P.O. Box 213
Philomath, OR
(541) 929–2433
www.peaktoport.peak.org
p2p@peak.org

Pilot Butte Challenge
Bend, OR
(541) 388–6055
www.oregonstateparks.org

Sunrise to Summit Race
Mount Bachelor
Bend, OR
(541) 388–0002
www.mtbachelor.com

OCTOBER

King of the Hill (12K)
West Linn, OR
(503) 497–4080
www.bigredlizard.com

McDonald Forest Cross Country Race
(15 K)
Peavy Arboretum
Corvallis, OR
(541) 758–8124
www.orst.edu/groups/triclub/ultra

Oktoberfest 10 Mile
Mount Angel, OR
(503) 497–4080
www.bigredlizard.com

Portland Marathon
1000 Southwest Broadway, Suite 1900
Portland, OR
(503) 248–1134
www.portlandmarathon.com
info@portlandmarathon.org

NOVEMBER

Clackamas Cross Country Classic (5K)
North Clackamas Park
Milwaukie, OR
(503) 646–7867
www.orrc.net

Kevin's Cup (8K Trail Run, 35-mile
Ultra Road Run)
Mary S. Young Park
West Linn, OR
(503) 497–4080
www.bigredlizard.com

DECEMBER

Ho Ho 5K
Cook Park
Tigard, OR
(503) 497–4080
www.bigredlizard.com

About the Author

Lizann Dunegan is a freelance writer and photographer and specializes in writing outdoor guidebooks and travel articles about the Northwest. Lizann has been running trails in the Northwest for more than ten years and is often accompanied by her partner, Ken Skeen, and her two border collies, Levi and Sage. Lizann also loves cycling, hiking, cross-country skiing, sea kayaking, and playing the violin and cello.

WHAT'S SO SPECIAL ABOUT UNSPOILED, NATURAL PLACES?

Beauty   Solitude   Wildness   Freedom   Quiet   Adventure
Serenity   Inspiration   Wonder   Excitement
Relaxation   Challenge

There's a lot to love about our treasured public lands, and the reasons are different for each of us. Whatever your reasons are, the national **Leave No Trace** education program will help you discover special outdoor places, enjoy them, and preserve them—today and for those who follow. By practicing and passing along these simple principles, you can help protect the special places you love from being loved to death.

THE PRINCIPLES OF LEAVE NO TRACE

- Plan ahead and prepare
- Travel and camp on durable surfaces
- Dispose of waste properly
- Leave what you find
- Minimize campfire impacts
- Respect wildlife
- Be considerate of other visitors

LEAVE NO TRACE OUTDOOR ETHICS

Leave No Trace is a national nonprofit organization dedicated to teaching responsible outdoor recreation skills and ethics to everyone who enjoys spending time outdoors.

To learn more or to become a member, please visit us at www.LNT.org or call (800) 332-4100.

Leave No Trace, P.O. Box 997, Boulder, CO 80306